VB

P9-EJJ-362

MIRACLE

Also by Danielle Steel

Danielle Steel

MIRACLE

Delacorte ▆ Press

MIRACLE
A Delacorte Book / July 2005

Published by
Bantam Dell
A Division of Random House, Inc.
New York, New York

Book design by Virginia Norey

Delacorte Press is a registered trademark of Random House, Inc.,
and the colophon is a trademark of Random House, Inc.

The jacket format and design of this book are protected trade
dresses and trademarks of Dell Publishing, a division of
Random House, Inc.

LIBRARY OF CONGRESS CATALOGING-IN-PUBLICATION DATA
Steel, Danielle.
Miracle/Danielle Steel.
p. cm.
ISBN 0-385-33633-0
I. Title
PS3569.T33828 M56 2004   2002041011
813/.54 21

Printed in the United States of America
Published simultaneously in Canada
www.bantamdell.com

BVG   10 9 8 7 6 5 4 3 2 1

To miracles,
large and small,
that bring forgiveness.
And to great loves,
oh so rare,
and hard won.

with all my love,
d.s.

"... all human wisdom was contained
in these two words: Wait and Hope!"

ALEXANDRE DUMAS
The Count of Monte Cristo

MIRACLE

1

THE SAILING YACHT *VICTORY* MADE HER WAY ELEGANTLY
along the coast toward the old port in Antibes on a rainy
November day. The sea was choppy, as Quinn Thompson
stood silently on the deck, looking up at the sails, savoring his
last few moments aboard her. He didn't mind the weather or
the gray day, or even the rough seas. He was an inveterate and
seasoned sailor. The *Victory* was a hundred-fifty-foot sailboat,
with auxiliary engines, that he had chartered from a man he
had done business with frequently in London. Her owner had
had business reversals that year, and Quinn had been grateful
to have use of the boat since August. He had used her well,
and the time he had spent aboard had been good for him in
every way. He was healthy, strong, and more peaceful than he
had been when the trip began. He was a handsome, vigorous,
youthful-looking man. And more than he had been in months,
he was resigned to his fate.

He had boarded the yacht in Italy, and after that spent time in Spanish and French waters. He had hit a traditionally rough patch in the Gulf of Lions, and relished the excitement of a brief and unexpected storm. He had sailed on to Sweden and Norway afterward, and returned slowly through several German ports. He'd been on the boat for three months, and it had served a useful purpose. It had given him all the time away that he needed, time he had used well to think and recover from all that had occurred. He had been stalling his return to California for months. He had no reason to go home. But with winter setting in, he knew he couldn't delay his return much longer. The owner of the *Victory* wanted her in the Caribbean for his own use by Christmas, as they had discussed when they agreed to the charter. Quinn had paid a fortune for three months aboard, but he didn't regret a penny of it. The stiff price of the charter meant nothing to Quinn Thompson. He could afford that, and a great deal more. Materially and professionally, he had been a very lucky man.

The time on board had also served to remind him of how passionately he loved sailing. He didn't mind the solitude, in fact he thrived on it, and the crew were both expert and discreet. They had been impressed by his skill, and quickly realized he knew far more about the *Victory,* how to sail her hard and well, than did her owner, who knew next to nothing. Above all, for Quinn, she had provided both a means of escape and a gentle haven. He had particularly enjoyed his time in the fjords, their stern beauty seemed to suit him far more than the festive or romantic ports in the Mediterranean, which he had assiduously avoided.

His bags were packed in his cabin as he stood on deck, and,

Miracle

familiar with the efficiency of the crew by then, he knew that within hours of his departure, all evidence of his time aboard would have vanished. There were six male crew members on board, and one woman, the wife of the captain, who acted as stewardess. Like the others, she had been discreet and polite, and rarely said much to him, and like the owner, the entire crew was British. And he and the captain had enjoyed a comfortable and respectful rapport.

"Sorry for the chop on the way in," the captain said with a smile as he joined Quinn on deck. But he knew by now that Quinn wouldn't mind. Quinn turned to nod at him, undisturbed by the waves breaking over the bow, and the rain beating down on them. He was wearing foul weather gear, and in fact, he liked the challenge of hard sailing, rough seas, and the occasional storm. The only thing he didn't like was leaving. Quinn and the captain had spent hours talking about sailing, and the places they'd been. And the captain couldn't help but be impressed by Quinn's extensive travels, and the depth of his knowledge. Quinn Thompson was a man of many hats and many faces, a legend in the world of international finance. The yacht's owner had told the captain before Quinn arrived that he had been a man of humble beginnings who had made a vast fortune. He had even gone so far as to call him brilliant, and after three months on the boat with him, the captain didn't disagree with that opinion. Quinn Thompson was a man whom many admired, some feared, a few hated, sometimes with good reason. Quinn Thompson was direct, sure, powerful, mysterious in some ways, and unrelenting about anything he wanted. He was a man of infinite ideas, endless imagination in his field, and few words, except when he was in one of his rare expansive moods, which the captain had enjoyed as well, usually after a few brandies. For the most part, they had kept their conversations confined to sailing, a topic that they both enjoyed, more than any other.

The captain knew Quinn had lost his wife the previous spring, and Quinn had mentioned her once or twice. There were times when a wistful look came over him, and some somber days in the beginning. But for most of the hours they stood beside each other on deck, Quinn kept his own counsel. The captain knew he had a daughter as well, because he'd mentioned her once, but Quinn seldom talked about her either. He was a man who was quick to share ideas, but rarely feelings.

"You ought to make Mr. Barclay an offer for the *Victory*," the captain said hopefully as the crew took down the sails, and he turned on the motor, glancing at Quinn over his shoulder as they headed into port. Quinn smiled in answer to the comment. His smiles were hard won, but when they came, they were well worth it. They lit up his face like summer sunshine. The rest of the time, and far more frequently, he seemed lost in winter. And when he laughed, he was a different person.

"I've thought about it," Quinn admitted, "but I don't think he'd sell her." Quinn had asked John Barclay before chartering her, if there was any chance he would, and Barclay had said only if he had to, and had admitted he would give up his wife and children before his sailboat, a point of view Quinn both understood and respected. He didn't repeat the comment to the captain. But in the past three months, Quinn had fallen in love with the idea of buying a boat. He hadn't owned one in years, and there was no one to stop him now.

"You should have a boat, sir," the captain ventured cautiously. He would have loved to work for him. Quinn was hard but fair, respectful, and exciting to sail with. He had done things with the *Victory*, and gone places, John Barclay would never have dared or dreamed of. The entire crew had loved the three months they had spent sailing for Quinn Thompson. And Quinn himself had been thinking of buying or building a boat since August, especially now that his months on the *Victory* were over. It would be the perfect answer to getting out of San Francisco. He had already decided to sell the house, and was thinking of buying an apartment somewhere in Europe. At sixty-one, he had been retired for nearly two years, and with Jane gone, he had no reason to stay in San Francisco. He realized that a boat might restore joy to his life. In fact this one already had. He hated the fact that people often disappointed each other. But boats never did.

"I've been coming to the same conclusion myself all morning," Quinn said quietly. He hated to leave the *Victory*, and he knew she was sailing in two days for Gibraltar, and after that to St. Martin, where her owner was meeting her for Christmas with his wife and children. The price Quinn had paid to charter her was helping Barclay to afford her, and had made an enormous difference. She would surely be his for at least another year as a result. "Do you know of anything comparable up for sale at the moment?" Quinn asked with interest, as the captain kept his eyes straight ahead, watching their course as they came into the channel, and he pondered the question.

"Nothing up to your standards, I suspect, not a sailboat." There were always large power boats changing hands, but fine sailboats of the caliber Quinn would want were harder to come by. In most cases, their owners loved them—and wouldn't part with them easily. He was still thinking about it when the first mate joined them, and the captain asked him the question, and Quinn was intrigued when the young man nodded.

"I heard about one two weeks ago, when we left Norway. She's not finished yet, but she's up for sale. She's still in a ship-yard in Holland. Bob Ramsay commissioned her last year, and he just decided to sell her. He wants a bigger one. I hear the one for sale's a beauty." All three men knew she would be if she had been commissioned by Bob Ramsay, he was a notable sailor with three handsome yachts he competed with in all the European races, and he generally took all the prizes. He was an American with a French wife and they lived in Paris. He was a hero in the international sailing world, and all the boats he had built were exquisite.

"Do you know which yard she's in?" Quinn asked, suddenly wondering if this was the answer to his prayers, as the young man brightened.

"I do. I'll call them for you, if you like, as soon as we dock."

Quinn was leaving on a flight to London that afternoon, spending the night at a hotel, and flying to San Francisco the next morning. He had called his daughter, Alex, in Geneva about seeing her before he flew home, and she had said she was too busy with the children. He knew the real reason for her not seeing him, and he no longer had the energy to fight it. The battles between them were too bitter and had gone on for too long. She had never forgiven him for what she perceived as his failures in her childhood. And she had told him months before that she would never, ever forgive him for calling her so late in her mother's illness. In fact, he realized now that blind hope and denial had kept him from calling her earlier than he had. Both he and Jane had refused to believe she would actually die. They kept telling themselves and each other that she would survive. And by the time Jane agreed to let him call their daughter, it was only days before the end. And even then they didn't think she would die. He wondered at times if he and Jane had wanted to be alone for her last days, and had unconsciously failed to include Alex.

When Alex had flown home to see her mother, Jane was ravaged. Alex had arrived two days before Jane died, and she was either in such extreme pain or so heavily sedated, Alex had hardly been able to speak to her mother, except in rare lucid moments when Jane continued to insist she would be fine. Alex had been numb with grief and shock, and blazed with fury at her father. All her misery and sense of loss had channeled itself into the resentment she already felt for him, and the flames of disappointment and grief and anguish were fanned into outrage. She sent Quinn one searing letter of agony as soon as she returned home, and for months after that she hadn't returned a single one of his phone calls. In spite of Jane's final pleas for them to make peace and take care of each other, Quinn had all but given up on Alex since his wife's death. He knew how distressed Jane would have been over their estrangement, and he felt badly about it, but there was nothing he could do. And in his heart, he thought Alex was right. Without meaning to, he and Jane had cheated her of enough time to say good-bye.

The phone call he had made two days before from the *Victory* had been one last futile attempt to reach out to her, and he had been met by an icy rebuff. There seemed to be no way now to bridge the chasm, and her anger over her childhood had smoldered for too long. For all the years he had been building his empire, he had spent almost no time with Jane and the children. She had forgiven him, Jane always understood what he was doing, and what it meant to him, and never reproached him for it. She had been proud of his victories, whatever they cost her personally. But Alex had come to hate him for his absences, and his seeming lack of interest in her early life. She had told him that on the day of the funeral, along with her fury at not having been warned of the severity of her mother's illness. And although she had her mother's fragile looks, she was as tough as he was—in some ways even more so. She was as unrelenting and unforgiving as he had often been in the past. And now he had no defense in the face of her ire. He knew she was right.

There was a tender side of Quinn that few knew, and Jane had always been certain of, a soft underbelly that he kept well concealed, and that she cherished, even when it was least visible. And while Alex had his strength, she had none of Jane's compassion. There was an icy side to her that even frightened Quinn. She had been angry at him for years, and it was clear she intended to stay that way, particularly now that she felt he had cheated her of her last days with her mother. That was the final blow to their relationship as father and daughter. And he realized now, in the face of Alex's accusations, that he had wanted Jane to himself for her last days, and hadn't wanted to share her with Alex. Terrified of Jane's death, he had clung to denial. There had been so much to say to each other, after all the years he'd been away, all the things he had never said to her, and never thought he had to. In the end, he had said it all to her, they both had. And it was in those last weeks that she shared all her journals and poems with him. He had always thought he knew his wife, and it was only at the very end that he discovered he hadn't.

Beneath her calm, quiet, bland exterior had lived a woman of boundless warmth and love and passion, all of which had been directed at him, and the depths of which he had never fully understood until far too late. More than anything Alex could accuse him of, he now knew that he could never forgive himself for it. He had hardly ever been there for Jane. He realized he had abandoned his wife even more than he had abandoned their daughter. Jane should have been as angry at him as Alex was, but all she had done was love him more, in his endless absences. He was deeply ashamed of it and consumed with guilt he knew he would suffer for a lifetime. It seemed an unpardonable crime even to him, and even more so now that he had read all her journals. He had brought them with him on the trip, and had been reading them for months, each night. And even more than the journals, her love poems sliced into him like scalpels and tore his heart out. She had been the most compassionate, forgiving, generous woman he had ever known, and she had been a treasure far greater than he had ever suspected. The worst of all ironies was that it was only

9

now that she was gone that he understood it. Too late. So much, much too late. All he could do now was regret his failures and her loss for the rest of his lifetime. There was no way to repair it, or make amends, or even atone for it, although he had apologized for it before she died. Worse yet, Jane had assured him he had nothing to regret, nothing to reproach himself for. She promised him that she had been happy with him for the years they shared, which only made his guilt worse. How could she have been happy with a man who was never there, and paid almost no attention to her? He knew what he had been guilty of, and why he had done it. He had been obsessed with his empire, his achievements, and his own doings. He had rarely thought of anyone else, least of all his wife and children. Alex had every right to be angry at him, he knew, and Jane had had every reason to hate him, and didn't. Instead she had written him love poems and was fiercely devoted to him and Quinn knew better than anyone how little he deserved it. In fact, he had dreams about it almost every night now. Dreams in which she was begging him to come home, and pleading with him not to abandon her, or forget her.

Quinn had retired the year before she died, and they had spent a year traveling to all the places he wanted to explore. As usual, Jane had been a good sport about following him wherever he wanted. They went to Bali, Nepal, India, the far reaches of China. They had gone back to places they both loved, Morocco, Japan, Turkey. They hadn't stopped traveling all year, and for the first time in years, grew ever closer to each other. He had forgotten how entertaining she was, what good company, and how much he enjoyed her. They fell in love all over again, and had never been happier together than they were then.

It was in Paris that they discovered how ill she was, and the seriousness of it. She had had stomach problems for months, which they both thought were a harmless by-product of their travels. They flew home after that and had it checked out again. And it was even worse than they thought, but even then, they had both denied it. He realized now from her journals that she had understood the severity of what ailed her before he did. But she remained convinced nonetheless that she would beat it. She had been suffering in silence for months before that, not wanting to spoil the traveling he wanted so much to do, and had waited so long for. She was upset because their coming home had meant canceling a trip to Brazil and Argentina. It all seemed so pointless now, and so empty without her.

Jane was fifty-nine when she died, and they had been married for thirty-seven years. Alex was thirty-four, and her brother Doug would have been thirty-six now, if he had lived. He died in a boating accident at thirteen, and Quinn realized now that he had scarcely known him. He had much to regret and repent for. And he had the rest of his life in which to do it. Jane had died in June, and now, as they sailed into port in Old Antibes, it was November. It had been an agonizing, interminable five months without her. And Quinn knew with absolute certainty that he would never forgive himself for having failed her. His dreams and Jane's journals were a constant reminder of his failures. Alex had long since tried him and found him guilty. He didn't disagree with her.

The captain came to Quinn's cabin after they docked, to

give him the information about the sailboat that was under construction and up for sale in Holland. He had just called the boatyard. He was smiling as he crossed the threshold.

"She's a hundred and eighty feet long, and she sounds like a beauty," he beamed. "She's a ketch, and the yard says there's been some interest, but so far no one's bought her. Ramsay only just decided to sell her." The two men's eyes met, and a slow smile spread over Quinn's face. It was the happiest the captain had seen him. For most of the trip, Quinn had seemed tormented. "Are you going to go and see her, sir?" the captain asked with interest. "I'd be happy to change your flight for you. There's a flight for Amsterdam half an hour after the one you were going to take to London."

Quinn couldn't believe what he was hearing. It was more than a little crazy. A hundred-and-eighty-foot sailboat. But why not? He could sail around the world for the rest of his life. He couldn't think of anything he would have liked better. He could live on the boat, and sail around to all the places he loved, and those where he hadn't been yet. All he needed with him were Jane's poems and journals. There was nothing else in the world now that mattered to him. He had read them again and again. Their crystal clarity and open love for him were like a blow each time he read them.

"How crazy is that?" Quinn asked the captain, as he sat back in a leather chair in his cabin, and thought about the hundred-and-eighty-foot sailboat for a minute. He felt it was more than he deserved, but it was all he wanted. Living on a yacht was the perfect escape route.

"It's not crazy at all, sir. It's a shame for a sailor like you not to have a boat of your own." He wanted to tell Quinn that he would love to work for him, but he didn't want to be intrusive. But if Quinn bought the boat, he had every intention of saying it to him. There was no love lost between him and John Barclay, the *Victory*'s owner. Quinn Thompson was just exactly the kind of man he wanted to work for, he was the consummate sailor. John Barclay ran the *Victory* like a houseboat, and had no real need for a seasoned captain. Most of the time, all they did was sit in port, or at anchor while they went swimming. "She's a year away from completion, maybe less, if you push them. You could be sailing her wherever you want by the end of next summer. Or at worst, a year from now, sir."

"All right," Quinn said, looking suddenly decisive. "Let's do it. Do you mind changing my flight for me? I can fly to London after I see her." He had no schedule to meet, no timetable to follow, no one to see or be with, and the past three months had proven to him what he had suspected. He wanted a sailboat. And there was no one to stop him now. "Do you mind calling and telling the yard I'm coming?" Quinn's eyes looked hopeful and bright.

"Not at all, sir. I'll speak to the yard owner, and tell him to expect you."

"I'll need a reservation at the Amstel. Just for tonight. Tomorrow, I'll go straight from the yard to the airport, and fly to London." It was an exciting decision, and if he didn't like the boat, he didn't have to buy her. He could even commission one of his own from scratch, but that, Quinn knew, would take longer. It would take at least two years to build a boat comparable to the one Ramsay had ordered, possibly even longer.

The captain made all the arrangements for him, and half an hour later Quinn shook hands with him and the entire crew, and thanked them for their kindness to him. He had left generous tips for each of them, and had written a sizable check to the captain. He promised to let him know how things turned out in Holland. And as he sped toward the airport in Nice in a limousine, Quinn felt the same anguish he had felt for months, wishing he could tell Jane what he was about to do, and what he hoped would happen in Holland. There was always something he wanted to share with her, something that reminded him with agonizing acuteness of how empty his life was without her. He closed his eyes for a moment, thinking of her, and then forced himself to open them. There was no point allowing himself to get sucked into the black pit of grief again. It had been a constant battle since June. But the one thing he did know, and believed with every ounce of his being, was that a sailboat was at least one way to flee the places he had been and lived with her that had become too painful for him. A sailboat was something for him to live for. He could never replace Jane with a boat. But he sensed, as they reached the airport, that she would have been pleased for him. She always was. Whatever he chose to do, she always supported him, and celebrated each and every idea he had, no matter how crazy it seemed to anyone else. Jane would have understood, better than anyone. She was the one person who would. The one person, the only person he knew, who had really loved him. More than he had ever known when she was alive, he knew now without any doubt, his entire life with her had been a love poem, just like the ones she had written and left for him.

14

2

THE PLANE TOUCHED DOWN AT SCHIPHOL AIRPORT IN Amsterdam at six o'clock, and Quinn took a cab to the Amstel Hotel. It was one of his favorite hotels in Europe. Its ancient grandeur and exquisite service always reminded him some-what of the Ritz in Paris. He ordered room service shortly after he arrived and found himself torn between missing the com-forts of the *Victory* and her crew, and excitement over the boat he was planning to see in the morning. He found it nearly im-possible to sleep that night with the anticipation of it. All he hoped now was that he would love it.

He slept fitfully, and was up and dressed by seven the next morning. He had to wait another hour for a car and driver to come, and passed the time by reading the *Herald Tribune* over breakfast. It was an hour's drive from the hotel to the boat-yard, and by nine o'clock, he was in the office of the owner of the shipyard, a powerfully built older man, with an ebullient style, who had the plans on his desk, in anticipation of Quinn's visit. He had heard of him, and read of him over the years, and the night before, he had made some calls, and done some careful research. He had a very clear idea of what Quinn was about, and knew of his incisive, and allegedly ruthless reputation. To those who crossed him, or failed him in some way, Quinn could be fearsome.

Quinn eased his long, lean frame into a chair, and his blue eyes seemed to dance as he went over the plans with the owner of the shipyard. His name was Tem Hakker, and he was a few years older than Quinn. Both his sons were in the office with them, and explained the plans in detail to Quinn. Both of the younger men were in charge of the project, and took a great deal of pride in it, with good reason. The boat was going to be spectacular, and Quinn had fresh respect for Bob Ramsay's genius as he listened. The giant sailboat seemed to have almost everything he would have wanted. Quinn had a few additional ideas, and made suggestions as they talked, which in turn impressed both younger Hakkers, as well as their father. Quinn's ideas were of a technical nature, which improved on Ramsay's initial concept.

"He's crazy to give up this boat," Quinn said as he went over the plans with them again. He was anxious to see the boat now.

"We're building him an eighty-meter," Tem Hakker said with pride. Two hundred and fifty feet. But the one they were discussing seemed vast enough to Quinn. It was everything he could ever have wished for, and all he needed.

"That ought to keep him happy," Quinn quipped easily, referring to the eighty-meter, and then asked to see the boat still under construction that Ramsay was selling. And when he did, Quinn stood in awestruck silence and whistled. Even the hull looked beautiful to him. There were already large sections of the boat completed. The main mast was going to stand a hundred and ninety feet tall, and she was to carry eighteen thousand square feet of sail. She was going to be a sight to behold when she was completed. Even in her unfinished state, she was, to Quinn, a creature of exquisite beauty. It was love at first sight, and he knew looking at her that he had to have her, which was how he did things. Quinn Thompson was a man of instant and almost always infallible decisions.

They spent an hour examining her, discussing changes Quinn wanted to make now that he'd seen her, and then he and Tem Hakker walked slowly back to his office. Hakker and Bob Ramsay had agreed on a price for her, and after a few rapid calculations, keeping in mind the changes Quinn wanted made, he quoted a price that would have made most men blanch. Quinn showed no emotion as he listened, and just as rapidly countered. There was a long silent pause, as Hakker looked at him and took the full measure of the man, and nodded. And as he did, he stuck out his hand and Quinn shook it. The deal was done, at an impressive price, but there was no question in either man's mind that the yacht was worth it. Both men were delighted. And Quinn told him he wanted it completed by August, which he knew was optimistic, but now that he had seen her, he could hardly wait to set off on his travels and life of escape aboard her. The months of waiting for her would seem endless, but the anticipation thrilled him.

"I was hoping you would agree to November. Or perhaps

we could have her ready for you in October," Tem Hakker said cautiously. Quinn Thompson drove a hard bargain.

In the end, after some discussion, they compromised on September. Or at least by then Tem Hakker thought she would be ready for sea trials. And with luck, she would be ready to sail away by the end of the month, or at the latest the first of October. Quinn said he would live with that, if he had to. And he had every intention of flying over to see the work in progress as often as he could, and hold them to the date they had agreed on. It was nearly a year away, and Quinn could hardly wait to sail her.

Quinn left the yard at noon, having written a hefty check, and he called the captain of the *Victory* before he left to tell him the news and thank him.

"Good job, sir," the captain said, sounding ecstatic. "I can't wait to see her." He had every intention of writing to Quinn after that, to broach the subject of a job with him, but he didn't want to do it over the phone. Quinn was already thinking of it himself.

He had a million details and plans on his mind now. And he waved at the Hakkers as he drove away. They were every bit as pleased with the deal as he was, perhaps even more so. A boat of that scope and magnitude was not normally as easy to sell as it had been to Quinn Thompson. He hadn't hesitated for an instant, and as he drove back to the airport to catch his flight, he knew he had a new home as well as a new passion. All he wanted to do now was sell the house in San Francisco, and do whatever work he needed to do, to do so. There were a few things he knew he had to clean up before he sold it. But his mind was full now with all the details of the boat. He knew it was going to be a new life for him, for whatever years he had left. And it was going to make going back to the empty house that much easier, or at least he thought so.

He had had a small sailboat years before, and had encouraged both of his children to learn sailing. Like her mother, Alex had hated it, and after Doug's death in a boating accident at a summer camp in Maine, Jane had finally convinced him to sell the boat. He never had time to use it anyway, and had acceded to her wishes. For more than twenty years he had been content to sail on other people's yachts from time to time, always without Jane, since she didn't like boats. And now suddenly a whole new world had opened up to him. It seemed the perfect scenario for his final chapter, and just the way he wanted to spend the rest of his days, sailing around the world on a boat that was better than any he had ever dreamed of. He was still smiling to himself as he boarded the plane to London, and he spent the entire night making notes about it in his hotel room. The prospect of his new boat had changed the entire mood and tenor of Quinn's existence.

As Quinn boarded the plane to San Francisco at Heathrow the next day, he realized that soon San Francisco would no longer be home to him. All he had left there were memories of Jane, and the years they had shared, and he could take all of that with him. Wherever he went, whatever he did, she would always be with him. He had her precious journals in his briefcase, and shortly after take-off he took one of her poems out to read it. He read it again and again, as he always did, and then sat staring out the window. He didn't even hear the flight attendant speak to him and ask him what he'd like to drink as she offered. He was lost in his own thoughts, until she finally caught his attention. He declined the champagne, and asked for a Bloody Mary, which she brought to him before serving anyone else. The seat next to him was empty mercifully, and he felt relieved, as he hated talking to people on planes. The flight attendant commented to the purser about him when she went back to the galley. She said he looked like someone important. But when the purser glanced at him, he said he didn't recognize him, and agreed that he was a good-looking man, but he didn't appear to be particularly friendly. In fact, he wasn't.

"Probably just another CEO, tired after a week of meetings in London." It was what he had been once upon a time, not so long ago. But now he was someone very different. He was a man with an extraordinary new sailboat. Neither of them could have imagined it as they looked at him, but more important, he knew it. It was the only thing he had in his life to be pleased about, as he flew toward San Francisco. His wife had died, his daughter hated him, or thought she did, his son had died years before. He was alone in the world with no one to love him, or care about what he did. And in a few hours, he would be walking into an empty house, the house he had shared with a woman he had thought he knew and didn't. A woman who had loved him more than he felt he deserved, and toward whom he felt both grateful and guilty. In fact, he was certain of how unworthy he was, as he read her poem again, and then slipped it back into his briefcase. He closed his eyes then, and thought of her, fighting to remember every detail of her face, her voice, the sound of her laughter. He was desperately afraid that the memories would slip away from him in time, but he knew they wouldn't as long as he had her journals. They were his last hold on her, the key to the mysteries he had never understood, nor cared to discover. The poems and journals, and his regret and love for her, were all he had left of her that mattered.

3

THE PLANE LANDED IN SAN FRANCISCO RIGHT ON TIME, and Quinn passed through customs quickly. Despite his long absence from the States, he had nothing to declare, and he looked somber as he picked up his valise and briefcase, and hurried outside with his head down. He wasn't looking forward to getting home to the empty house, and he had realized with a pang on the plane, that he had managed to time his return to just before Thanksgiving. It hadn't even occurred to him when he made his plans, but he had no choice anyway. His charter of the *Victory* had come to an end, and he could no longer come up with a valid reason to linger in Europe, particularly if Alex refused to see him.

She had been polite but firm. Her outbursts at him had occurred before and after the funeral. And since then, any contact he'd had with her had been distant, formal, and chilly. In her own way, she was as stubborn as he was. She had been furious with him for years anyway. She and her mother had discussed it endlessly, and despite all of her mother's efforts to soften her point of view, Alex had continued to maintain her harsh, judgmental position. She claimed her father had never been there, for any of them, not even when Doug died. Quinn had come home for three days for the funeral. He'd been in Bangkok, concluding a business deal, when he got the news, and turned around and left again the morning after the funeral, leaving eleven-year-old Alex and her mother to grieve and mourn, and cling to each other in their solitary anguish.

He had been gone for a month that time, putting together an enormous deal that had made headlines in the *Wall Street Journal*, returned briefly again, and then took off to spend two months in Hong Kong, London, Paris, Beijing, Berlin, Milan, New York, and Washington, D.C. Now that she was an adult, Alex said she could hardly ever remember seeing her father, let alone talking to him. Whenever he was home, he was too busy, exhausted and jet-lagged, and sleep-deprived, to spend time with her or her mother. And in the end, he had managed to cheat her of even a decent amount of time to say good-bye to her mother. Quinn had heard it all before, during, and after the funeral, and would never forget it. There was no turning back from what she'd said and the bitter portrait of him she had painted. And the worst of it was that, as he listened to her, Quinn knew without a doubt that he couldn't deny it. The man she described was in fact the person he had been then, and was until he retired. And whatever changes had occurred since then, most of them positive, Alex was not willing to acknowledge.

Quinn had tried to make up to Jane for the long years when

he'd been busy and absent, and thought he had in some ways, as best he could, during the year and a half they had shared after he had retired. But there was no way he could make it up to Alex. It was also noticeable to him that she had married a man who scarcely left home, except to go to the office. She had married a Swiss banker right after college. They had gone to Yale together, and married almost minutes after they graduated, thirteen years before. They had two boys, lived in Geneva, and Quinn had commented to Jane right from the first that it was Alex who told Horst what to do, and what she wanted. They were inseparable, and seemed happy, sedate, and secure, though uninspired and unexciting. Quinn found his son-in-law painfully boring. Alex had been careful not to fall into the same trap she thought her mother had. Instead, she had married a weak man, to do her bidding, as different as possible from her father. Horst rarely, if ever, traveled, and worked in the bank his grandfather had founded. He was a responsible young man, who loved his wife and sons, and had no great ambitions. Alex had known when she married him that she would never be sacrificed to his career or accomplishments or passions. To Quinn's practiced eye, Horst had none. He simply existed, which was what Alex had wanted.

Her sons were six and nine, two beautiful little blue-eyed towheads, just like their mother, and Quinn scarcely knew them. Jane had gone to Geneva frequently to visit them, and Alex had brought the boys to San Francisco once a year to visit her mother, but Quinn had rarely been around when they came to town, and he always seemed to be in some other part of the world when Jane went to Geneva. Often, when Quinn was away, Jane took the opportunity to visit her daughter. Looking at it in retrospect, it was easy for him to see why Alex was angry. And she had no intention of letting her father make up for it, or atone for his sins, both real and perceived. As far as Alex was concerned, she had lost not one, but two parents. Quinn had died in her heart years before she had lost her mother. And the trauma of losing her brother when she was eleven years old had remained an open wound for her. It made her particularly protective of her children, despite her husband's pleas to give them just a little more freedom. Alex was convinced she knew better. And more than anything, because of her brother's accident, she hated sailboats.

Jane had never been fond of them either, but Quinn suspected she would have been happy for him, about the new boat he was building. Jane had always wanted him to be happy, to fulfill his dreams, and to achieve everything he had wanted to accomplish. Alex no longer cared what he did. As a result, Quinn was a man with no family, no ties to anyone, he was as solitary as he looked as he stepped out of the cab on Vallejo Street in a cul-de-sac filled with trees that all but obscured the house he and Jane had lived in for their entire marriage, and that Alex had grown up in. He had wanted to buy a bigger one as his fortune grew, but Jane had always insisted she loved this one. And Quinn had too while Jane was still there to come home to. Now, as he turned his key in the lock of the big rambling English-style house, he dreaded the silence.

As he stepped into the front hall and set his bags down, he could hear a clock ticking in the living room. The sound cut through him like a knife, and felt like a heartbeat. He had never felt as alone or as empty. There were no flowers any-where, the shades and curtains were drawn, and the dark pan-eling in the living room, which had once glinted and shone, now made the room look tomblike. He couldn't remember the house ever seeming as dark or as depressing. And without thinking, he went to the windows, pulled back the curtains, opened the shades, and stood staring into the garden. The trees and hedges were still green, but there were no flowers, and it was a dark November afternoon.

The fog had come in while they were landing, and it was swirling through the city. The sky looked as gray as he felt, as he picked up his bags and walked upstairs. And when he saw their bedroom, it took his breath away. She had died in his arms in their bed five months before, and he felt a physical pain as he stared at the bed, and then saw her smiling in a photograph next to it. He sat down on the edge of the bed, with tears rolling down his cheeks. It had been a mistake to come home, he knew, but there was no one else to sort through her things, and his own, if he was to sell the house in the spring. And he knew there was work to do on the house. Everything was in good or-der and worked well, but thirty-seven years in one house was almost a lifetime. He felt he had to organize the work and sort through their things himself, no matter how painful. Some of the rooms needed a coat of paint, and he wanted to consult a re-altor to find out what he had to do to sell it.

It was a long hard first night home for him, and he longed for Jane with such loneliness and agony that at times he wanted to run into the street in his pajamas, just to flee it. There was no escaping. He knew he had to face it. There was no

27

reprieve. His life without her was his sentence. Life without parole. He knew his solitude was forever, and felt he deserved it. And that night, he had the same dream he had experienced frequently before he left on his travels. It was a dream in which Jane came to him, held out her arms, pleading with him, and she was crying. At first the words were indistinct, but even without them, the look on her face tore his heart out. And then the words would come clear to him, and they were always the same, with subtle variations. She would beg him not to leave her, not to abandon her again. And each time he had the dream, he promised her he wouldn't. And then like a nightmare, not a dream, he would see himself pick up a suitcase and leave anyway, and all he could see after that was her face, crying after he left her. He could still hear her sobs when he woke up, at whatever hour, and her words would echo in his head for hours afterward, "Quinn, don't leave me...Quinn, please..." her arms outstretched, her eyes devastated. And whenever he woke from that dream, he felt panicked. How could he have done that to her? Why had he left so often? Why had his own pursuits always seemed so important? Why didn't he listen?

The dream entirely dismissed the reasons for his trips, and swept away the empire he was building. And all that was left afterward, in the dream, was his own crushing sense of guilt and failure. He hated the dream, and the fact that it had returned almost immediately, as soon as he came back to San Francisco. There was something so tragic about Jane in the dream, although in real life she had been tenderly empathetic and understanding, and had never reproached or implored him the way the woman in the dream did. Quinn hated the dream, and in some ways, he knew that guilt was the chain that bound him to her, as much as love had. But the fact that the dream had returned with a vengeance the moment he got home did not cheer him. It was a burden he knew he had to live with.

The next morning, he showered, shaved, dressed, swallowed a cup of coffee, rolled up his sleeves, and began digging into closets. He was still trying to get the dream out of his head, and felt haunted by it. He began with the easy closets downstairs, where Alex had stored all the mementos of her childhood. Jane had been urging her to take them for years, but she preferred to leave them with her parents. There were ribbons and trophies from her horseback riding days, and a few for tennis tournaments she'd been in, in college. Endless photographs of her friends, most of whom Quinn didn't recognize, from kindergarten to college. There were tapes, and home movies, a few battered old dolls, and a teddy bear, and finally a box at the back that he wrestled toward him. It was sealed and he used a penknife to open it, and when he did, he found that it was full of photographs of Douglas, many with Alex. The two of them laughing and smiling and cavorting, several of them skiing, and a whole pack of letters from him, when he had gone to camp in Maine, and she had gone to one in California, closer to home. And as though directed to by angels' wings, Quinn found himself opening a brittle, yellowed old letter, and he saw with a start that the date was the one on which Doug had died. He had written to Alex only that morning, hours before the sailing accident that had ended his life at thirteen. Tears streamed down Quinn's face as he read it, and suddenly he realized what they had all felt afterward, what he hadn't allowed himself to feel. In spite of the fact that he had loved his son, he had kept him at a distance. Quinn had barely allowed himself to know him.

Doug had been a handsome boy, happy, kind, intelligent, and looked just like his father, but Quinn had always put off getting closer to him. He had always thought they'd have time "later." He had fantasized their becoming friends as men, and instead the boy had slipped right through his fingers. And even then, he hadn't properly grieved him. It had been too painful to admit that he had missed the chance to know Doug better. And once again, guilt had consumed him, and he had fled so as not to face it. Each reminder of the lost child was like a silent accusation. In fact, he had insisted Jane put Doug's things away as soon as possible, and strip his room. Quinn had thought it would be too painful for her to leave Doug's room intact and treat it as a shrine. He had left for Hong Kong and insisted that everything be packed and gone before he came home the next time, supposedly for her sake. And dutiful wife that she had been, she had done it, just to please him, at God only knew what cost to her.

Quinn found almost everything that had been in the boy's room the following afternoon, when he went through a large storeroom behind the garage. It was all there, even his clothes, his sports equipment, his trophies and other memorabilia. She had saved every single thing, right down to his underwear.

Miracle

Twenty-three years later, she had saved every bit of it, and he even found three of Doug's sweaters tucked away at the back of Jane's closet, when he began taking things apart upstairs.

It was a sentimental journey that enveloped him for weeks. Again and again, he found himself confronting memories and realizations about himself, and Jane, that were excruciatingly painful and made him feel even more guilty.

Thanksgiving came and went, and he dutifully called Alex on the holiday, although she didn't celebrate it in Geneva. Her responses to him were brief and cursory. She thanked her father for calling, in a voice that was icy cold, and Quinn was so put off by her, he didn't even ask to speak to Horst or the boys. Her message was clear. Stay away. We don't need you. Leave me alone. So he did.

He didn't bother with a turkey, since he had no one to share it with, and he did not even bother to let any of their friends know he was back in the city. As painful as his mission was to weed through their belongings and sell the house, it would have been even more painful, he thought, to socialize with people. Jane had been his link to the social world. It was she who kept in touch with everyone, who loved to entertain their friends, and gently encouraged Quinn to slow down for a moment, and enjoy a quiet evening among people they knew well. And most of the time, he had done it for her. But without her softening influence and warmth, he preferred his solitude. He was alone now, and would forever stay that way. He had no interest whatsoever in seeing anyone. It would only make her absence more acute, and more painful, hard as that was to imagine.

By day, he was going through her closets, her treasures, her memories, and his own. And at night, he sat in bed, exhausted, reading her journals and poems. He felt as though he was steeped in her essence, like a marinade he was soaking in, until everything she had thought, felt, breathed, kept, loved and cherished was now a part of him, and had seeped into his skin. She had become his soul, as though he had never had one of his own before, and now theirs had joined and become one. He had never felt closer to her than in those final months before her death. And now again, as he waded through everything she'd owned, not only her papers, but her evening gowns, her gardening clothes, the faded nightgowns that she slept in, her underwear, her favorite sweaters. And as she had done with her son's sweaters hidden at the back of her closet, Quinn found himself putting things aside to save, the things that had meant the most to her. He could barely bring himself to part with any of it, and now he understood only too well what it must have done to her when he had insisted she take apart Doug's room. Life had finally turned the tables on him, and he felt that what he was experiencing now was suitable punishment for everything he had done to her. He embraced the task with reverence and humility, and accepted it as the penance he deserved.

It was mid-December before he had brought some semblance of order to what was left, and had decided what to throw away and what to keep. There were piles of things to give away, or box and store, all over the living room. And it was still too big a mess to call a realtor in. His only distractions were the calls to Tem Hakker every week to check on the progress of the boat they were finishing for him. Quinn had had a nice letter from Bob Ramsay by then, congratulating him on his new acquisition. He was also delighted to be off the hook, and free to pursue his much larger new sailboat. According to the Hakkers, things were going well, and on schedule. For the moment, taking apart the house in San Francisco seemed a much bigger job to him, but Quinn was glad he was doing it himself. It gave him some sort of final communion with Jane, a sacred ritual that he could perform that kept her close to him. And every night, he read her words, in her firm, slanting hand. More often than not he dreamed of her afterward. And two or three times a week, he had the dream where she begged him not to leave her. Even by day, he felt haunted by it.

He had come across thousands of photographs of them, from the early days when the children were small, on their travels, at important occasions, and more recent ones from their last trips. And she had kept every single newspaper article that ever mentioned him. Nearly forty years of them put away in files and boxes, some of them so frail that they fell apart when he touched them, but all of them organized chronologically. She had been meticulous in her respect and admiration of him. So much more than he had been of her. Seeing his accomplishments described in the clippings, he realized again and again how selfish he had been, how totally absorbed in his own world, while she loved him from afar, waited for him to come home, forgave him everything, and made excuses for him to the children. She was an admirable woman.

Although he was not a churchgoer, Quinn went to church on Christmas morning and lit a candle for her. He did it mostly because he knew it would have meant something to her, and she would have been pleased. She had lit thousands of candles for Doug over the years. And whenever anything worried her, or she had some special concern, she went to church and lit candles. He had teased her about it, and now he was surprised to find a strange sense of peace steal over him as he did it for her. As though the warmth and bright glow of the tiny candle would somehow make a difference in some unseen way. And then he went home, feeling slightly relieved. The things he was donating were in boxes by then. Those he was keeping were in sealed cartons piled up in the garage. He was going to put them in storage at some point before he left, along with whatever furniture he was keeping. They had had some fine antique pieces, and if nothing else, he thought he should keep them for Alex. He doubted that he would ever have a home where he would use them again. If all went according to plan, he had every intention of living on his new boat for the rest of his days, once it was ready.

On Christmas night, he finally indulged himself. It had been a hard month since his return. He drank most of a bottle of fine old red wine he had found in the wine cellar, polished it off with two brandies, and went to bed. And he felt better for it, despite the hangover he had the next day. He was glad that the holidays were almost over. He spent New Year's Eve at his desk, going over papers that his attorney was going to file in probate court after the first of the year. He worked for hours, as he listened to a driving rain battering his windows, and he

34

could hear the wind whistling through the trees. It was midnight when he finally got up and glanced outside, and saw that the slimmer trees were being pressed almost level to the ground with the gale force of the wind. He didn't bother to turn the television on, but if he had, he would have discovered that it was the fiercest storm to hit northern California in more than a century, and there were power lines down all over Marin County and the East and South Bay.

He was in bed and sound asleep in the dark house, when he heard a tremendous crash outside, followed almost as quickly by two more. He got up and glanced out the window again, and saw that the biggest tree in his garden had fallen over. He went outside in his pajamas and a slicker to look at it in amazement, and saw instantly that it had sheared off a corner of the roof when it fell. And when he walked back into the house and stood in his living room, there was a gaping hole open to the sky, as the rain poured in. He needed a tarp to cover it, but didn't have one. All he could do for the moment was move the furniture out of the way so it wouldn't be ruined by the rain. He had been unable to determine what the other two crashes had been. The rest of the trees around the house were swaying violently in the wind, but none of the others had fallen, and the rest of the house appeared to be undamaged, until morning.

He had been unable to sleep for the rest of the night, as he listened to the storm raging around him, and it was still raining the next morning, when he got up at first light, he put on boots and his slicker again, and took a walk around the house to survey the damage. The hole in the roof was ugly, several of the shutters had been torn off, and two big windows were broken. There was glass and debris everywhere, and the garage had been severely damaged and was flooding. By sheer luck, he had put all the boxes to store on long wooden tables, so none of their papers and mementos had been destroyed. But he spent the rest of the morning moving them into his kitchen. The living room looked like a disaster area. He had moved the rugs and furniture in the middle of the night, and set down tubs and towels to catch the rainwater coming in through the hole in the ceiling. It was a part of the living room that protruded beyond the rest of the frame of the house, and there was a branch coming through it, and some of the fine old paneling had splintered from the impact. He learned from the newspaper that morning that at least a dozen people had been killed, mostly by fallen power lines, or trees, and hundreds had been injured around the state. Thousands were temporarily homeless and huddled in school gymnasiums as lowlands flooded. It was a storm of mammoth proportions.

And as he made one more trip from the garage to the kitchen, carrying a large box, he saw what must have caused the second and third crashes the night before. Two trees had fallen in his neighbor's garden. They were smaller than the one he had lost, but had nonetheless done considerable damage when they fell. There was a small woman with dark hair, looking mournful and dismayed as she assessed the destruction, and she happened to glance up at Quinn as he walked past her.

"Mine came right through the roof at four o'clock this morning," he said cautiously. "I heard two more crashes, it must have been your trees going down," he observed, and the woman nodded. And none of them were small trees, it was very impressive. "How bad is the damage?"

"I'm not sure yet. It looks pretty nasty. The house is leaking like a sieve, and I've got Niagara Falls in my kitchen." She looked frightened and worried. Quinn didn't even know her name, he knew the house had sold just after Jane died, but he had never met the family who bought it, and had never been interested in who they were, and still wasn't. But he felt sorry for her. She seemed to be dealing with it on her own, and it made him think of Jane, who had handled anything and everything, and every possible crisis and disaster on her own, in his absence. He assumed this woman's husband was of the same breed as he had been, a man with a job that took him far from home on New Year's. At least half of the New Year's Eves of their marriage Quinn had spent alone in other countries in hotel rooms. And obviously, this woman's husband was no different.

"I've got some spare buckets, if you need them," Quinn offered helpfully. There wasn't much else they could do on New Year's Day, and it was easy to figure out that every contractor in the state would have his hands full by Monday morning.

"I need a roofer. I just moved in, in August, and they said the roof was sound. I'd love to send them a picture of the kitchen. It looks like someone turned on the shower." The storm had also broken nearly half her windows. The house was even more exposed than Quinn's was, and less solidly constructed. It had changed hands several times in the past dozen years, and Quinn paid no attention to who lived there, although Jane always made some small effort to welcome new neighbors. But he had never seen this one, or her husband, even in passing. She had a faintly desperate look as she tried to clear away some branches. It was still pouring rain and the wind was still ferocious, though not quite as vicious as it had been in the early hours of the morning. The damage looked like what he'd seen in the aftermath of hurricanes in the Caribbean, or typhoons in India. It was definitely not what one expected to experience in San Francisco.

"I'm going to call the fire department and get them to put a tarp on the roof. Do you want them to take a look at yours too?" he offered. It seemed to be the least he could do, and she nodded gratefully, looking wet and distracted. The damage all around them was upsetting, and all up and down the street, people were doing what they could to clear away fallen trees, pick up debris, and tie down what they could to minimize further damage, as the storm continued raging.

"I'm not sure a tarp will make much difference," she said, looking unhappy and confused. She had never had to handle a situation like this. Nor had Quinn, and he somehow felt that Jane would have been far more efficient than he was. But he had to manage on his own now.

"They'll tell you what you need. I'll ask them to bring several tarps, just in case." And as an afterthought, he remembered his manners. "Sorry," he said, reaching a wet hand over a low hedge, as he juggled a box in his left arm, "I'm Quinn Thompson."

"Maggie Dartman," she said, shaking his hand firmly. She was small, and had tiny, graceful hands, but her handshake was strong. She had long dark hair that hung down her back in a braid, and her hair was matted against her head in the driving rain. She was wearing jeans and a parka, and looked soaked to the skin, and he couldn't help feeling sorry for her. She was very pale, and had big green eyes that looked anything but happy. He couldn't blame her, he wasn't pleased with the damage to his house either.

"Bad luck your husband's not around," he said sympathetically, making an easy assumption. She looked to be in her late thirties or early forties, and there were no children afoot, which made him wonder if she was even younger, and hadn't started a family yet. These days everyone got started older. She looked at him oddly when he mentioned her husband, started to say something, and then didn't. And a moment later, Quinn left to call the fire department. They had had hundreds of calls like his, and said they would be over in an hour or two to cover the hole in his roof. He dutifully mentioned his neighbor, and told her the fire department would be over to help, when he went back to get the last box in the garage, and saw her dragging a branch out of her driveway.

"Thanks very much," she said, and nodded. She looked like a drowned rat, and he was tempted to offer her an old raincoat of Jane's he was sending to Goodwill, but didn't. There was no need to get too friendly. She seemed polite, but she was also reserved, and a moment later, she went back into her house. He wasn't sure, but as he saw her go, he thought she was crying. He wondered how many times Jane had cried when she had to cope with emergencies without him. And as Quinn went back into his own house, thinking of it, he felt guiltier than ever.

4

THE FIRE DEPARTMENT COVERED THE HOLE IN QUINN'S roof, and as he had promised, he directed them to check on his next-door neighbor. By late that night, the storm abated, but the damage throughout the state had been tremendous. Like everyone else in town, he called a contractor on Monday morning, and a roofer. He found their names on a list Jane kept on a bulletin board in the kitchen. The roofer just laughed when Quinn called him.

"Let's see," the man said, sounding harassed but good-natured. "You're the forty-eighth call I've had this morning. I think maybe I can get to you sometime in August."

"I hope you're joking," Quinn said drily. He was not amused. He was also not used to dealing with problems like this. Whatever happened around the house, even something of this magnitude, would have automatically been Jane's problem. Now it was his, and he had to admit he didn't enjoy it. He had dialed the roofer and the contractor more than a dozen times each before he got through to either of them. Everyone who'd suffered damage in the storm was obviously frantic to get someone to repair it as quickly as they could, and he was no different.

"I wish I were joking," the man at the roofing company responded. "There's no way we can do it." He gave Quinn four names to try, all reputable firms, he said. And the contractor did the same when Quinn called him. He gave him the name of two well-known contracting firms, and a third number that he said was a young carpenter who had gone out on his own a few months before, but did fine work, and he highly recommended him. Predictably, the two contracting firms were as busy as the first one. He still hadn't found a roofer yet, and feeling exasperated, Quinn called the young carpenter the first contractor had recommended. Quinn was beginning to realize that getting the repairs done was going to be far from easy.

There was an answering machine at the number when he called, and he left a concise description of the damage, explaining what had happened. And the last roofer he called agreed to come and take a look the following morning, but he warned Quinn when they spoke that there were a good six or eight weeks of work ahead of him by then. It looked like Quinn was going to be living with a hole in his living room ceiling and a tarp over it for a long time. This was not the way he had planned to spend his final months in San Francisco.

It was eight o'clock that night when the young carpenter finally called him. He sounded matter-of-fact and businesslike, and apologized for the hour of the call. He said he'd been out looking at storm damage since early that morning. Quinn was just grateful that the man had called him. He offered to come by at seven the next morning if it was all right with Quinn.

"I'm doing a quick job for a friend tomorrow. All their bedroom windows broke, and they have a brand-new baby. I'd like to come by and see you on the way there, if you don't mind my coming that early. I want to get his windows taken care of before I start any big jobs."

"Are you already booked by anyone else?" All day Quinn had been hearing that people had three to six months of work lined up from the storm, and he was beginning to feel desperate. He couldn't even think of selling the house until he repaired the damage the storm had done.

"Not yet. I saw eight or nine potential clients today, but I haven't signed any contracts yet. I don't like to take on more work than I can handle. And a lot of people feel more comfortable with bigger firms, where they know they can count on big crews. I have three subs I use when I need them, and whenever possible I do the work on my own. I keep better control of the job that way, and it keeps the prices down, although it's a little slower going, but not much. I don't have to correct anyone's mistakes that way. Why don't we take a look in the morning and see what I can do for you, Mr. Thompson?"

"Sounds good to me," Quinn said, feeling relieved. He would have met him at five in the morning, if he had to. He liked the way the man sounded. He sounded straightforward and sincere, honest and responsible. His name was Jack Adams. And then Quinn told him about the trouble he'd had, understandably, finding a roofer.

"I've got a good guy I work with in San Jose. I'll call him

tonight and see how booked up he is. He might be able to come in for a couple of weeks. I'll let you know what he says tomorrow."

"Perfect." Quinn thanked him and hung up. It would be wonderful if he could put the whole job in this man's hands, and trust him to take care of it for him. He might even be able to do whatever else was necessary to get the house in shape to sell it.

Quinn went to sleep that night, in the bed he had shared with Jane, and for once he didn't read her poems and journals. He went straight to sleep, after thinking about getting the house in shape again, and hoping that Jack Adams was the man to do it.

He woke at six, feeling refreshed, put on jeans and a heavy sweater, socks and boots, and went downstairs to make himself a cup of coffee. He had just finished his second cup, when Jack Adams rang the bell at seven o'clock sharp. He looked neat and clean and well organized. He had short dark hair, and big blue eyes that looked honest and friendly and kind. Quinn offered him a cup of coffee, and he declined, he wanted to get down to business as quickly as possible, and give Quinn an idea of what he felt he could do to help him. He had liked Quinn on the phone, and the two formed an instant bond, as Quinn led him from the living room to the garage, and all around the house wherever something had been broken, loosened, destroyed, or damaged. He didn't carry a pad and pen with him, which worried Quinn, but as they moved along, he seemed to remember every detail of what they had just seen, and shot his mental list back at Quinn with amazing accuracy

44

and precision. If his work was as good as his mind was sharp, Quinn felt certain that, by sheer luck, he had found a winner.

Jack Adams was a nice-looking young man, somewhere in his mid-thirties. He was as tall as Quinn, and as lean, and there was an odd similarity between them as they walked around the house, and through it, but neither of them was aware of the physical resemblance between them. To passersby, they would have looked like father and son. Although Quinn's hair was gray now, it had once been as dark as Jack's, and they had the same frame, and the same way of moving, almost the same gestures as they discussed the problems and the repairs to be done. In fact, Jack was almost the same age as Douglas would have been. He was thirty-five years old, and Doug would have been thirty-six. And he looked very much the way Doug might have looked if he'd grown up into manhood. It didn't even occur to Quinn as the two men were talking. In his mind's eye, Doug had stayed forever thirteen.

"How long do you think it will take?" Quinn asked him pointedly as they walked back into the house again, and this time Jack accepted a cup of coffee. There was more to do than he'd anticipated, and Quinn had talked to him about additional work, if he'd take it on, so he could get the house in shape to sell it. There were a dozen other jobs he'd been offered since the storm, but he liked the idea of sticking with one job and completing it, and some of what Quinn needed him to do was challenging. His friend in San Jose had agreed to do the roof, and was scheduled to start in two days, and Quinn had been enormously relieved to hear it. What Jack did was inspire confidence and give his clients the sense that he had everything well in hand. Both the self-assurance he exuded and his obvious expertise made Quinn want to secure his services as quickly as possible, if Jack was willing.

"All of it?" Jack narrowed his eyes, thinking about it, and then took a sip of the steaming coffee Quinn handed him. "I'd say, three months, maybe two, depending on how many guys I use. There are two I'd like to have with me on this job, at least in the beginning. I can finish up the loose ends myself, depending on how much work you want me to do to help you sell it. Maybe all three of us for the first two months, and then either one or two of us for the last month. How does that sound to you?" Jack asked fairly.

"That sounds about right to me. Will you oversee the roofer too?" Quinn had no desire to become the job foreman on the project, but Jack had no intention of letting him do that, and there was no need to. He was totally competent, and the men he used liked working for him.

"I'll take care of everything, Mr. Thompson. That's my job. All you do is write the checks. And I'll keep you apprised of what we're doing." Jack was well spoken and intelligent, and there was an instant respect between the two men. Quinn needed his help, and badly, and he knew it. And from everything Jack had seen of Quinn, he liked him. Jack had a sense that Quinn would be fair with him. He was a businessman, and probably a good one, to the very tips of his fingers. You could see easily that he was used to being in command, and Jack also sensed correctly that Quinn didn't want to be bothered with the details. As far as Jack was concerned, he didn't need to be. He wondered if there was a wife he was going to be dealing with too. There were a number of photographs around of a pretty, middle-aged woman, but Quinn hadn't mentioned her. He was handling the matter himself, maybe just because it was easier for him to do it. But whatever his circumstances, Jack didn't feel they were any of his business, and didn't ask any questions of a personal nature. Quinn liked that too. Jack Adams was all about business, just as he was.

"How fast can you work up an estimate?" Quinn asked matter-of-factly. In the hands of any of the larger firms, Quinn knew it would have cost him a fortune. But this man was young and independent, and hopefully not insanely expensive. Quinn didn't think he would be. Jack wanted the work, and seemed excited about the prospect of working for him.

"I can have it to you by this afternoon," Jack responded as he set down the mug and glanced at his watch. He wanted to do the job for his friend that day so he would be free to do this one. "If it's all right with you, I'll drop it by this evening. I have a friend who does some of the paperwork for me. It leaves me free to get out in the field and do what I need to do. I'll call the numbers in to her today, and bring it to you when I finish work. Will that work for you?"

"Perfectly. You can have her fax it to me if that's easier for you." He handed Jack the fax number on a piece of paper, and Jack stuck it in his pocket, and held out a hand to Quinn.

"I hope we'll be working together, Mr. Thompson."

"I hope so too," Quinn said simply, and smiled at him. He liked everything about him, his look, his manners, how bright he was, what he had said about the work to be done. Jack Adams was the best thing that had happened to him since the storm that hit San Francisco.

Jack left a few minutes later, and drove off in his truck.

Feeling immensely relieved, Quinn went to put in a call to Tem Hakker in Holland, to check on the progress of his sailboat. And he couldn't help wondering, as strange as it may have seemed, if Jack liked sailing, or knew anything about boats.

5

JACK ADAMS CAME BACK, AS PROMISED, THE NEXT DAY
and the work began in an orderly, efficient way. He had faxed
Quinn a very reasonable estimate, as promised, the day before.
The deal had been made, and a contract signed. He brought
two big burly young men with him, and they kept to themselves and went straight to work. They greeted Quinn, or nodded, when he went in or out, but Jack was the only one who
had contact with him. And the roofer appeared to do his work
at the end of the week. The tree had done more damage than
they'd thought at first, and the roofer consulted with Jack and
Quinn about what needed to be done. It was an extensive job,
but Quinn had no choice in the matter. The roof had to be repaired, and Quinn wasn't trying to cut corners. He wanted it
done right, in the best possible way, no matter how expensive
it was, even though he was selling the house. And Jack respected him for that, as he did for all else. He had already figured out in the first few days that Quinn Thompson was a

pleasure to work with, as long as you were fair with him, and told him honestly what was happening, and what you thought you could do about it. What he didn't like were misrepresentations and lies, or people who shirked their responsibilities. But there was none of that with Jack Adams in charge of the job. He was completely professional, and every few days, he brought Quinn up to speed.

He was coming into the house to do just that at the end of the second week, when he found Quinn sitting at his desk and poring over some plans.

"Building a new house somewhere?" Jack asked pleasantly. He never asked questions inappropriately, but Quinn was so intent on what he was looking at that Jack couldn't help but be intrigued. And whatever the plans were for, it looked huge.

Quinn looked up with a tired smile. He had done a lot of paperwork for Jane's estate that week, and it was tedious, depressing work. His reward to himself for doing it was spending some time going over the latest plans for the boat. "Not a house, Jack. A boat. Do you know anything about boats?"

"Not a thing," Jack admitted with a grin. "I've looked at them a lot, and watched some sailboat races on the bay. But I've never been on a boat in my life."

"You're missing a great thing," Quinn said, as he turned the plans around on his desk, so Jack could see them. He knew he would appreciate the precision with which they had been done. Jack was meticulous himself. "She'll be ready in the fall. I'm going to live on her, after I sell this house." Jack nodded, looking the plans over carefully. He didn't ask questions, he was just admiring what he was seeing.

"Where are you going to sail the boat to?" Jack asked with interest.

"Everywhere. The South Pacific. Antarctica. South America. Europe. Scandinavia. Africa. I can go anywhere I want with a boat like this. I bought her in November, the day before I came home from Europe."

"She must be beautiful to see," Jack said admiringly, but without a touch of envy. He had a great deal of respect for Quinn, and thought the man deserved all he had.

"Not yet, but she will be when she's finished."

"Where is she?" Quinn was amused when he asked the question. The name of the boatyard was written boldly across the page, with the word NETHERLANDS printed out clearly, but Jack had obviously not seen it. Quinn assumed he had been too dazzled by the boat's exquisite design to notice, and he couldn't blame him. Quinn was already deeply in love with his new boat, and he was sure that anyone who would see her would be too.

"She's being built in Holland," Quinn answered.

"Do you go over often?" Jack was intrigued by him. Everything about Quinn suggested style, elegance, and power. He seemed like a real hero to him.

"I will until she's finished. I want to oversee the details myself."

"When are you putting the house on the market?" They had talked about it, and Jack was aware of it, but Quinn hadn't given him any precise dates. Now that he had seen the plans for the boat, Jack knew that Quinn's departure was not vague or simply a possibility, it was real.

"I'll put the house up for sale as soon as you're finished, or sometime in late spring. I'm assuming it will take a few months to sell. I want to be out of here by September or October. The boat should be ready by then."

"I'd love to see her. I hope you bring her here." But that was exactly what Quinn didn't want. He wanted to get as far away as he could from his relentless memories, and the world he had shared with Jane. All he wanted now was to sail away and take his memories with him. Being in the house he had shared with her, in the city where they had lived for nearly forty years, was just too hard for him. He hardly slept at night, and roamed throughout the house, aching for her. Thinking about all the things he had never done for or with her was a heavy weight to bear. What he needed now was a reprieve, and he felt certain the boat would give that to him. Jack knew that Quinn's wife had died. Quinn had mentioned it to him one day the previous week, and Jack had told him quietly how sorry he was to hear it. He sensed now some small measure of how lonely Quinn was. Quinn had also said that he had a daughter who lived in Geneva.

"Maybe you'll come to Europe and see the boat one day," Quinn suggested as he put the plans away. Jack laughed in answer, and told him a trip to Europe was as foreign to his world as a rocket ship ride to outer space, and about as likely for him.

"I think I've got enough to keep me busy here. But that certainly is a handsome boat," he said respectfully, and as he did, Quinn had an idea. He strode across the room to a bookcase where he had an entire library of sailing books, some very old and some quite rare. He took a heavy volume out and offered it to Jack. It was an introduction to sailing that Quinn had used as his bible for years in his earliest sailing days.

"This will teach you everything you'd ever want to know about sailboats, Jack. You might enjoy it sometime in your free time." Jack hesitated as Quinn held it out to him.

"I'd hate to lose it or damage it." The book looked much loved and well worn, and possibly even valuable. He was obviously uncomfortable about borrowing it.

"I'm not worried about it. See what you think, you can return it when you're finished. You never know, you might have a chance to go sailing with a friend one of these days. This book will teach you everything you need to know." Jack took it slowly from him, and flipped through some of the sketches and pictures. There were diagrams and sailing terms throughout. It was a wonderful book that Quinn had always loved. He had given it to Doug to read that fateful summer before he left for camp, and Doug had pored over it, and memorized parts of it in order to impress his father, and had. It had been one of their few great exchanges and precious moments before he died.

"You're sure you want to lend it to me?" Jack asked, looking worried. Quinn smiled and nodded, and a few minutes later, Jack left with the book under his arm. And although it was Friday night, he had mentioned that he would be back in the morning. His crew were only working for him five days a week, but he had already told Quinn he would be putting in some weekend hours on his own, and it was all part of their contracted price. He liked working alone sometimes, and getting a handle on some of the details himself. He was even more conscientious than Quinn had thought he would be, and the work was going well. He was supervising the roof work too, and Quinn was pleased with the results, although there was still a lot of work to do. Jack was going to be around for months, until the house was not only in good repair, but ready to put on the market.

On Saturday morning, Quinn looked out the window when he got up and saw Jack outside. It was raining again, and had been for most of the month. But Jack didn't seem to mind. He was used to working in the elements, and the only problem the rain represented for them was that they couldn't finish the roof until the weather was dry. The wet weather was drawing things out. But there were plenty of other projects at hand.

Quinn went outside to talk to Jack after he read the paper and had coffee, and he found him in the garage. He was checking on the repairs they'd been forced to do out there, and as the two men walked out of the garage half an hour later, chatting casually, Quinn noticed his neighbor struggling to open an enormous crate someone had delivered in front of her house. And as she had been before, after the storm, she was once again wrestling with it herself. She never seemed to have anyone to help, and as Quinn watched her, he thought of Jane once again, with a familiar pang. In all those years, he had never once thought about how difficult life must have been for her, with him gone all the time. And now he never seemed to stop thinking about it. This woman was a living reminder of the life Jane had been challenged with during all of his working life.

And as Quinn thought of it, Jack eased through the hedge

that separated the two houses, and went to help her. He took the tools from her hand, and within minutes he had the crate open, and offered to take its contents, a piece of furniture, inside. Before Quinn could say anything, they disappeared into the house, and a few minutes later, he was back. Jack was cautious when he mentioned her to Quinn.

"I don't know how you feel about it, Quinn." They called each other by their first names by then, and Quinn was comfortable with it. He liked everything he knew about Jack, and above all the fastidiousness and devotion with which he worked. "She asked me if I could do some work for her sometime. I told her I had a long job here, and she asked if I could do a few repairs for her on Sundays, if I have any spare time. I don't really mind, it's my day off, and I get the feeling she really needs the help. I don't think she has a man around."

"People probably used to say that about my wife too," Quinn said with a sigh. "Don't you need some time off? You can't work seven days a week, you'll wear yourself out," he said with a look of concern. He wasn't crazy about the idea of Jack working for her. He worked hard, and needed some rest, at least on Sundays, since he worked extra hours for Quinn on Saturdays.

"I think I can handle it," Jack said with an easy smile. "I feel kind of sorry for her. I was talking to the mailman the other day, he says her son died last year. Maybe she needs a break and a helping hand." Quinn nodded. He couldn't argue with that. And he made no comment, sympathetic or otherwise, about her son. He hadn't told Jack about Doug. There was no reason to, and Quinn thought it sounded maudlin. It was enough that he knew Jane had died. But he and the neighbor had something in common, not that it was something he wanted to talk about.

"I don't mind. Just don't let her take advantage of you, Jack," Quinn warned, and Jack shook his head. He was willing to help her, he wasn't being forced. And she had managed to find a roofer on her own, and gotten the work she needed done. But she said there were a number of smaller repairs she hadn't found anyone to tackle yet. And like Quinn, she had observed how diligent and competent Jack was about his work.

"She seems like a nice woman. Sometimes you just have to put out a hand, even if it costs you some time. I've got nothing else to do on weekends except watch football." It was more than Quinn had to do, but he didn't say that to Jack.

And the following day, he noticed Jack going in and out of Maggie Dartman's house. She stopped and said something to Quinn a little while later, as she was going out, and thanked him for allowing her to use Jack's services on his day off.

"He's a great guy," Quinn reassured her, not wanting to get involved in their arrangement. It was entirely up to Jack what he did in his spare time, and by midafternoon, Quinn noticed that Jack's truck was gone. He really was a decent man.

It was the end of the following week when Quinn remembered the book he'd given him, and asked Jack if he'd had time to read it yet. Jack looked slightly embarrassed and shook his head, and apologetically explained he hadn't had time.

"I can see why, between working here six days a week, and doing extra duty at my neighbor's," Quinn pressed him a little bit, good-naturedly, and Jack rapidly changed the subject.

Miracle

Quinn sensed that he felt guilty he hadn't read the sailing book yet, and he didn't want to put pressure on him. He had just thought he might enjoy it, but the poor guy was working himself to the bone on both jobs, particularly Quinn's. He didn't know why, but he had the feeling that Jack could be a born sailor if he wanted to. He had shown such interest in the plans for the boat, and teaching him something about sailing was something Quinn could do for him. He hoped he'd read the book at some point, and not just say he had, but he forgot to mention it again.

It was late January and the work was going well, when Quinn spent an entire afternoon making a list of extra projects he had for Jack, and comments about the work in progress, and he went outside to hand it to him. It was the first really sunny day they'd had in weeks, and the roof work was finally finished, although it had taken longer than planned. He wanted Jack's comments on the list he'd made, and stood waiting for him to read it, as Jack folded it and put it in his pocket, and promised to read it that night, which irked Quinn a little bit. He hated putting things off, and wanted to discuss it with him, but Jack said he had too much going on that afternoon to concentrate on it properly. He promised to discuss it with Quinn the next day when he came in.

But that afternoon, the work having gone particularly well that day, and hating the lull that came on Friday nights when everyone left, Quinn asked him in for a glass of wine, and he mentioned the list to Jack again, and suggested he take it out of his pocket, and they go over it together. Jack hesitated, and tried to brush it off, as Quinn insisted. He was like a dog with a

57

bone about his list, and for an odd moment, Quinn thought he saw tears shimmer in Jack's eyes, and wondered if he had offended him. Jack was generally easygoing and unflappable, even when things went wrong on the job, but he was obviously upset by Quinn's suggestion, so much so that Quinn was afraid he might quit, and that worried him acutely.

"Sorry, Jack," he said gently, "I didn't mean to press you, you must be dog tired by the end of the week. Why don't you skip tomorrow?" he suggested, trying to pacify him and back down from the pressure he had provided, apparently too much so for Jack. But Jack only looked at him and shook his head, and this time the tears in his eyes were clear. The look he gave Quinn was one of deep sorrow and immeasurable trust, and Quinn didn't understand what was happening. Just looking at Jack upset him. It was as though something in the younger man was unraveling, and could no longer be stopped. And out of nowhere came an explanation that Quinn was in no way prepared for, as Jack quietly set down his glass of wine. He looked straight at the man who had hired him, and spoke in a voice rough with emotion, as Quinn watched him, and listened with an aching heart. He had meant no harm with his questions and suggestions, but he could see that he had hurt this man whom he had come to respect and like. It was one of those moments when you can't go back, only forward. Like a pendulum swinging only forward, and never back.

"My parents left me at an orphanage when I was four years old," Jack quietly explained. "I remember my mother, I think I do anyway, I don't remember my father, except I think I was

Miracle

scared of him. And I know I had a brother, but I don't remember him at all. It's all kind of a blur. And they never came back. I was state-raised, as they say. They put me in a couple of foster homes at first, because I was so young, but they always sent me back. I couldn't be adopted because they knew my parents were alive somewhere, and you can't stay in foster homes forever. I got comfortable in the orphanage, and everyone was pretty good to me there. I did okay. I worked hard. I started doing carpentry when I was about seven. And by the time I was ten, I was pretty good. They let me do what I wanted, and I did whatever I could to help out. And I hated school. I figured out early on that if I did work at the orphanage, they'd let me skip classes, so I did, a lot. I liked hanging out with the grown-ups better than the kids. It made me feel independent and useful, and I liked that. And by the time I was eleven or twelve, I hardly ever went to school. I stuck around, going to school when I had to, till I was about fifteen. And by then, I knew I could make a living as a carpenter, so I took one of those high school equivalency tests. To tell you the truth, a friend helped me take it, a girl I knew. I got my diploma, and I left the orphanage and never looked back. It was in Wisconsin, and I had a little money saved up from jobs I'd done. I hopped a bus and came out here, and I've been working ever since. That was twenty years ago. I'm thirty-five now, and I make a good living at what I do. I work hard, and I like it. I like helping people, and working with someone like you. No one's ever been as nice to me as you are, not in all these twenty years." His voice cracked as he said it, and Quinn's heart ached for him as he listened, but he still had not understood. "I'm a carpenter, Quinn, and a good one. But that's all I am. That's all I'll ever be, all I've ever been. That's all I know how to do."

"I didn't mean to push you, Jack," Quinn said gently. "I admire what you do a lot. I couldn't do it. You have a real talent for finding solutions and making things work." And Quinn had noticed that he had a knack for design as well.

"Maybe not," Jack said sadly, "but you can do a lot of things I can't, and never will."

"I've been lucky, and worked hard, like you have," Quinn said, offering him the kind of respect that grows sometimes between two men, no matter what their origins or how simple or complicated their field. Quinn Thompson was a legend, and Jack Adams was a carpenter, and a good one, as he said, and an honest man. Quinn didn't want more than that from him. But Jack wanted a great deal more for himself, and he knew he would never have it. The burdens of his past were too heavy, and he knew it, better than Quinn could imagine. Quinn had no concept of the life Jack had led, or the path he had followed to get there.

"You're not lucky," Jack said quietly. "You're smart. You're educated. You're a lot better than I am, and you always will be. All I can do is this." He said it with total self-deprecation.

"You can go to college, if you want to," Quinn said hopefully. There was a sense of despair about Jack that he had never seen before in the month he had worked for him. He had always been so matter-of-fact and so cheerful, but what he was seeing now was very different. It was a glimpse into Jack's heart and soul, and the sorrow he had concealed there for a lifetime. If nothing else, Quinn wanted to give him hope.

"I can't go to college," Jack said with a broken look, and then looked straight into Quinn's eyes. Quinn knew he had never seen such trust. "I can barely read," he said, and then dropped his face into his hands and cried quietly. The shame of a lifetime spilled over and devoured him, as Quinn watched, feeling helpless. And without a sound, he reached toward him and touched his shoulder, and when Jack looked up at him again, it brought tears to Quinn's eyes too. He was sure now that no one, in his entire life, had admitted anything as important to him. This man whom he scarcely knew, but liked almost like a son, had dared to bare his soul. It was a precious gift.

"It doesn't matter," Quinn said, still touching him, as though his hand on the young man's shoulder would keep the connection between them, and it did.

"Yes, it does. I can't read books, or letters, or your lists. I don't know what it says at the post office, or what the forms say at the bank. I can't read a contract. I took an oral test at the DMV. I can read signs, but that's about it. I can't read what it says on medicine bottles, or directions, and maps are hard for me. I can hardly read anything. And I can sign my name. That's it. I'll never be more than a carpenter who can't even read. I can't even stay with a woman for more than a few weeks, because if they figured it out, they wouldn't want me. They'd think I was stupid, or ridiculous. All I can do is what I do, the best I can. But that's all I can ever do, or ever will."

It was instantly obvious to Quinn that Jack wanted so much

more out of life, but had no idea how to achieve it. His eyes were full of sorrow and the limitations he had lived with for a lifetime as he looked at Quinn. And what he had said was so overwhelming that Quinn didn't know what to say to him at first. He wanted to put his arms around him and hold him, as he would a child. But Jack wasn't a child, he was a man, and as decent and kind and capable as any man Quinn had ever known. He wanted to help him, but he wasn't sure how. All he could do was accept him, and try to let him know that whether he could read or not, he had won Quinn's respect forever, particularly now. His grip on Jack's shoulder remained powerful and firm. And a few minutes later, Jack stood up, and said he had to leave. He looked embarrassed by the admissions of the night, and Quinn could see that Jack looked shaken.

"I have a friend who reads things to me," Jack said softly, as he picked up his jacket. "I'll know what's on your list by tomorrow," he said simply, as Quinn nodded and watched him go. It had been a moment Jack had allowed Quinn to share with him, a glimpse not only at his vulnerabilities, but into his very soul.

Quinn lay in bed thinking about him that night, until three o'clock, deeply moved by what Jack had shared. And when he woke in the morning, and saw Jack's truck outside, he pulled on a pair of pants and a sweater, slipped his feet into loafers, and walked outside to find him. The two men exchanged a long look that spoke volumes, and Quinn asked him to come inside with him. Jack looked as tired as Quinn felt. He had lain awake for hours too, wondering if he had done the right thing in telling Quinn. And in fact, he had. His greatest fear, the one that had kept him up all night, was that of losing Quinn's respect.

"I memorized the list," he said to Quinn, as they stepped into the house and Quinn closed the door. He nodded and walked into the kitchen, as Jack followed, and both men sat down.

"I need you to put in some extra hours," Quinn said quietly, and Jack couldn't read what he was seeing in Quinn's eyes. There was no mention of what had been said the night before. "I want you to stay two hours after work every night, and maybe an hour or two on Saturday too." He sounded stern as he said it, although he didn't mean to, and Jack looked worried. There had been nothing about that on the list.

"You don't think the work is going fast enough?" Jack inquired. It was going faster than he'd expected, and he had assumed Quinn thought so too.

"I think the work is going fine. But we have some additional work to do." Quinn's heart was beating faster as he said it. This was important, and he wanted Jack to agree to do it, for both their sakes. It was as important to Quinn now as it was to Jack. They had formed a partnership the night before, a silent contract, a bond that could not be broken. Jack had given him something precious when he trusted Quinn with the truth. And Quinn was going to honor it, and felt honored, to his very core.

"What kind of work?" Jack asked, looking puzzled.

There was a long pause as the two men looked at each other. There was something very naked and raw in the room. It was hope. "If you'll let me," Quinn began cautiously, "if you'll allow me the privilege of doing so, I'm going to teach you how to read." There was a deafening silence in the room, and Jack turned away from him, with tears pouring down his cheeks. And Quinn was crying too. It was a long time before Jack turned to look at him again, and longer before he could speak.

"Do you mean that? Why would you do that for me?"

"Because I want to, we both do. I've done a lot of dumb, stupid, mean, selfish things in my life, Jack. This might turn out to be the first decent thing I've ever done, and I'd appreciate it if you'd give me that chance." It was Quinn asking Jack for something, both of them had much to gain from it, not just Jack. It was a journey they were both embarking on, to an unknown destination. "Will you do it?" Quinn asked him, and slowly Jack nodded, and dried his face with his hand.

"Are you kidding?" Jack smiled slowly, and his expression of jubilation was mirrored in Quinn's eyes. Jack had wanted to attend a literacy program all his life, and had been too ashamed. But he felt nothing shameful about learning to read with Quinn now. All he felt was pride. "When do we start?" He beamed.

"Now," Quinn said quietly, pulling the newspaper toward him, and pulling his chair around so he could sit next to Jack. "By the time you finish this job, you're going to read better than anyone I know. And if it takes longer than the work you're doing here," Quinn reassured him, "that's okay too. There was a reason you told me what you did last night, for both of us. Now let's see what we can do." Jack smiled up at his teacher, and Quinn poured them each a cup of coffee and sat down again. The lessons had begun.

6

THE READING LESSONS WENT WELL FOR THE FIRST FEW weeks. Jack spent his days working on the repairs on the house. And for two hours afterward, and sometimes more, he and Quinn sat at the kitchen table and wended their way slowly and painfully through the newspaper. Eventually Quinn used his old sailing book as their textbook, once Jack was more comfortable. They were a full month into it, when Quinn shared with him one of Jane's simple, lovely poems. It was a victory when Jack not only got the meaning of it, but was able to read it slowly and smoothly out loud. And when he did, he looked up at Quinn in amazement.

"That's beautiful. She must have been quite a woman," he said softly, still moved by what he'd read, and thrilled that he had been able to read it at all.

"She was," Quinn said sadly. "I didn't always know that about her. I only discovered who she was in the last months we spent together. I don't think I ever really knew her before."

He had learned even more about her, through her poems and journals once she was gone. The tragedy was that for thirty-six years before that, he had barely known her, and much of the time, took her for granted or ignored her. It was an admission he had only recently come to accept about himself, and not one he was proud of.

"She looks beautiful in the photographs," Jack said quietly. She had been a delicate, almost fragile-looking woman, but there had been far more strength in her than anyone ever suspected, least of all her husband. And her spirit had been gentle and graceful to the core.

"She was beautiful," Quinn admitted. It was easy for Jack to see now how much Quinn had loved her. "She was a remarkable woman," he added with a wistful look, as they wound up the lesson.

Jack was making impressive progress, and Quinn was giving him something he had always dreamed of. In a way, it was a gift of freedom, and one by one Quinn was helping him to sever the chains that had bound him. His inability to read had been like a death sentence to him, or at the very least a lonely prison. It was Quinn who was imprisoned now, condemned to his own loneliness and bitter recriminations forever. He was still having the recurring dream, but less often ever since he'd started helping Jack with his reading. It was almost as though doing something for another human being was helping to assuage his guilt.

It was late February, when they were finishing their lesson on a Saturday, that Jack mentioned Quinn's neighbor, Maggie Dartman. He was still doing work for her on Sundays, and slowly fixing the house that had been in serious disrepair when she bought it. But each time he worked for her, he was struck by how lonely she was. Her house was full of photographs of her son who had died. She had told Jack the boy had committed suicide two days after his sixteenth birthday. She never explained why, and it was obvious to Jack by then that there was no man in her life. The work he was doing for her could have been done by any man in residence, if there had been one to help her out. She had mentioned to him once that she was a teacher, and had been on sabbatical for a year and a half, since her son died.

Quinn and Jack had fallen into an informal tradition of having dinner together on Friday nights, after they finished his reading lesson. Quinn cooked and Jack brought wine, and it was an opportunity to get to know each other better. At times the relationship was one of friendship between two men, and at others Quinn took a fatherly attitude toward him. Jack was fascinated by Quinn's accomplishments. He had grown up on a farm in the Midwest, and had gone to college with a scholarship to Harvard. And from there he had progressed rapidly into his enormous success. Jane had believed in him from the moment she met him. She had been there before he ever made a penny, and never doubted his abilities for a minute. Success had come early for him, and bred more success. He had made his first million before he was twenty-five. He had had the Midas touch, as they said in the financial world. To the uninitiated, it looked like he had never made a bad deal in his life. But the truth was that when he had, he had managed to turn it into something better. And he always knew instinctively when to cut his losses. He was, in his own way, a genius. But from all Jack could see, success hadn't brought him happiness. There were few men as unhappy and solitary as Quinn Thompson.

And all Quinn wanted now was to become even more solitary, as soon as his boat was ready. He talked to Jack about it like a woman he was in love with and waiting for. It was all he dreamed of now. After being abandoned by Jane when she died, and the torturous relationship he had with his daughter, the boat being built for him in Holland was a nonthreatening companion of sorts who couldn't torment or reproach him, and whom he in turn could not disappoint or hurt. Being alone on the boat, isolated from the world, would be an immense relief. And while he waited for her, he was helping Jack to find his dreams.

There was much about the friendship that they both treasured. And while Jack was getting to know Quinn better, at the same time, with his weekly visits, he was growing extremely fond of Maggie. There was something so kind and vulnerable about her. She usually made Jack lunch on Sundays when he worked for her. And like Quinn, perhaps for similar reasons, she seemed desperately lonely. He seldom saw her go anywhere. She was always in her house, reading or writing, or just sitting and thinking. He saw her face whenever she passed one of her son's photographs, and the look in her eyes tore Jack's heart out.

"You should invite her over sometime," Jack finally suggested to Quinn. "She's a nice woman. I think you'd like her."

Quinn looked instantly upset at the suggestion. "I'm not interested in meeting women. I had the best there was. I'm not going to date anyone. It would be disrespectful to Jane, and a travesty to her memory." Quinn already knew he would never betray her. He had hurt enough people in one lifetime and had no desire to hurt more. But Jack was quick to clarify his suggestion, and surprised by how sensitive Quinn was.

"I didn't mean like that, Quinn," Jack corrected the impression he had given him. "She's a nice person, and she's had some tough things happen to her. I don't know all the details, but losing a son would be enough to bury most people. I don't think she sees anyone. She never goes anywhere, the phone doesn't ring. I never see friends come to visit her. It might just be nice to have her to dinner on a Friday sometime. She has a nice sense of humor. It would be an act of kindness. She doesn't look like she's interested in meeting anyone either." From things she had said to him, Jack had accurately guessed her state of mind. She was living with her memories and regrets as much as Quinn.

"I thought she was married." Quinn looked surprised. "I assumed she had an absentee husband who was away on business."

"So did I at first. She just looks that way, and it's a big house for a single woman. She must have a little money. I don't know if she's widowed or divorced, but whatever she is, she's alone in that house day after day. Maybe her husband died too, and left her some money." The house was substantial, and couldn't have been inexpensive when she bought it, despite the somewhat shabby state it was in. And she seemed cautious about how much she spent to repair it. She always discussed with Jack how much things would cost her. "I don't know her story,

Quinn, but whatever it is, I don't think it's a happy one. I think you'd be a good Samaritan if you invite her over to have dinner with us some Friday after work."

"Yeah, maybe," Quinn said vaguely. But two weeks later, when he pulled an enormous veal roast out of the oven, Jack looked at him in dismay.

"Even I can't eat all that, it's a crime to waste it." Rather than shrinking, for once the roast seemed to have grown exponentially when Quinn put it in the oven. It had turned out to be a lot bigger than he expected, and was an experiment of sorts. It was the fanciest meal he had prepared since they had begun their Friday night dinners. "Do you want me to call Maggie and see what she's doing?" Quinn hesitated, looking less than enthusiastic about it, and then reluctantly relented. Jack seemed to be determined to include her, and Quinn was beginning to wonder if Jack had a romantic interest in her.

"All right, it can't do any harm, I suppose. Tell her it was your idea. I don't want her to think I'm pursuing her, or interested, or that this is some ploy to introduce us. Tell her I'm a disagreeable old recluse with an oversize veal roast to share with her." Jack laughed as he went to the phone and called her. She sounded startled, and as hesitant as Quinn had been. She asked Jack bluntly if it was some kind of a setup, and if it was, she wasn't coming. He assured her that it was nothing more than a Friday night dinner shared by three friends, two of them neighbors. Finally, she agreed to come, and rang Quinn's doorbell ten minutes later with a cautious expression.

When he opened the door to her, Quinn was startled by how much smaller she was than he had remembered. They had chatted with each other over their respective hedges. But standing on his doorstep, she looked not only fragile, but tiny. And there was something in her eyes that gave Quinn the impression she was both frightened and sad. If nothing else, it made him want to reassure her. He could see why Jack felt sorry for her. She was a woman who looked as though she needed to be protected, or at the very least needed a friend.

He stepped aside and invited her in, and she followed him quietly to the kitchen, where Jack was carving the veal roast. She brightened visibly the moment she saw him. The smile that lit her face made her seem instantly younger. And Quinn relaxed the moment they sat down, and he handed each of them a plate, and filled their glasses with wine.

"How are the lessons going?" she asked comfortably, after thanking Quinn for inviting her to join them. Jack had confessed to her what they were doing every day after work, and how grateful he was to Quinn. Maggie had said he must be a nice man.

"It's coming, slowly, but surely," Jack said as he smiled at her. But in truth, he was making good progress. He was able to read clearly now, though very slowly, and some words still stumped him. He had all the sailing terms down now, but was anxious to move on to broader concepts. Quinn was desperate to teach him about sailing as well as reading. He wanted to share that with him, as it was his passion. And Jack was growing anxious to read other books as well. Quinn had also shared many of Jane's poems with him, which touched Jack profoundly. They were lovely and obviously heartfelt.

"He's a star pupil," Quinn said proudly, and Jack looked

slightly embarrassed. "Jack tells me you're a teacher," he said to Maggie, as he served dessert and made coffee.

"I was," she said easily, enjoying their company more than she had expected. They were a motley crew, drawn together by proximity, circumstances, and good intentions. "I haven't taught in nearly two years." She looked a little wistful as she said it.

"What did you teach?" Quinn asked with interest. He could easily imagine her surrounded by very young children, maybe kindergarten.

"Physics, in high school," she said, and surprised him. "The subject everyone hated. Or actually, they didn't. Most of my students were fairly gifted. They don't take physics unless they have a knack for it. If not, they opt for biology or calculus, or integrated sciences. Most of my students went on to major in physics in college."

"That means you did a good job with them. I always liked physics in college. I never took it in high school. What made you stop?" he asked casually, and was startled and saddened by her answer.

"My son died. Everything came to a grinding halt after that," she said honestly. There was no artifice about her, and Quinn liked that. "He committed suicide nineteen months ago." She could have told them in days or weeks, but no longer did that. She hated the fact that it was months now, and soon it would be years. Time was slowly creating an un-governable distance between them. She couldn't control it, just as she had been unable to control his actions in the end. "He suffered from severe depression. Most depressed kids don't

72

commit suicide, even if they think about doing it. Usually, it's more bipolar kids. But Andrew couldn't pull out of it. He pretty much lost his grip once he got to high school. I just didn't have the heart to go back to school once he died. They gave me compassionate leave to do some grief counseling. And after I did, I realized I wasn't ready to go back. I'm not sure I ever will be." But sooner or later, she knew she had to work, at something, if not teaching.

"What do you do now instead?" Quinn asked quietly.

Maggie sighed before she answered. "I've started counseling other parents like me. I'm not sure I'm a big help to them, but at least I've been there. And three nights a week I work for a suicide hotline for teenagers. They call-forward a line to me, and I can do it from home. I'm not sure if it's a good thing or not, but at least I feel like I'm doing something to help someone, instead of just sitting home and feeling sorry for myself."

Quinn wondered if that kept the wound open for her, but in spite of a look of sorrow in her eyes, she seemed to be a fairly well-balanced person. He wondered where her husband was, but didn't want to ask her. She volunteered the information a short time later on her own.

"I probably would have gone back to work by now, but Andrew's death kind of unsprung my marriage. I think my husband and I blamed each other for what we couldn't change or stop. Things had been shaky between us for a while, and in the year after Andrew's death, the marriage fell apart completely. He walked out two days after the anniversary of Andrew's death. Our divorce was final the week after Christmas." She said it in a strangely matter-of-fact voice, as Quinn realized that

that was when he first met her, and an instant later, she confirmed what he had thought. "I got the papers in the mail the day the storm hit on New Year's Eve. The storm seemed like a suitable end to all of it. I must have seemed like a crazy person the day I talked to you," she said apologetically. "I'm not even sure I was coherent. I was pretty upset."

"You seemed fine to me," Quinn said reassuringly, remembering her standing in the pouring rain without a raincoat or umbrella. There had been something devastated in her face when she told him she had Niagara Falls in her kitchen. And now he understood it better. She seemed to have no need to hide what she was feeling, and he suspected that she felt better now. Better enough to come to dinner at least, and he was suddenly glad that Jack had pressed him to invite her. More than anything else, this woman needed friends to distract her. They were like three souls in a lifeboat. And for the moment, Quinn was rowing. And he suddenly decided to share something with her, if only to let her know that she was not alone in her agony, and would survive it.

"My son died twenty-three years ago, in a boating accident," he confided as he set his fork down and looked at her across the table, as Jack watched them. He had never heard that from Quinn before, and was deeply touched by the admission. The only child Quinn had mentioned to him was Alex, in Geneva. "He was thirteen, and I think I only realized recently how deeply it changed both of us. I withdrew even deeper into my work, and my wife became more introverted and stayed that way. We were both grief-stricken, but when I read her journals, after her death, I understood better how profoundly it altered her. I was busy then, and probably insensitive about it. I'm sure I wasn't much help to her. It was too painful for me to talk about, so I seldom, if ever, did. She wrote some beautiful stories about him." There were tears in his eyes as he spoke, and he didn't confess to her that he had forced Jane to put away Doug's things within weeks after he died. And the little she had kept unboxed, she had concealed from Quinn in her closet. In a sense, he had forced her to do that, and now that he understood what it had meant to her, he deeply regretted what he'd said and done. He had thought he was doing the right thing for her, for himself, and even for Alex. But now he knew he'd been wrong. He had learned so much about her and himself in the months since she'd been gone.

"It's not a great thing to happen to a marriage," Maggie said, looking at Quinn. Her eyes bored into his like drills, as though asking a thousand questions. She wanted to ask him how he had survived it, or how his wife had. She still blamed herself for the end of her marriage.

She had always felt that her husband had lacked empathy for the depths of their son's depression, and that perhaps unknowingly, because of it, he had exacerbated Andrew's desperation. And because of that, she had never forgiven Charles for Andrew's death, and he knew it, whether she said it or not. He in turn felt she should have been able to stop it. Their final year together had been one of relentless silent accusation, until they could no longer stand each other. And no matter what they did to each other or themselves, nothing would bring their son back. Although she was devastated when Charles left, she felt he had made the right decision for both of them. In the end, their marriage had been as dead as their son. Charles had given her the best settlement he could, in the form of the house he had paid for her to buy, to escape the one where their son died, and he had given her enough money to live on for the next few years. Eventually, she'd have to go back to teaching. But for the moment, she was still hiding, as Quinn was. He understood that much about her. She had wrapped herself in a cocoon, to protect herself from the realities and blows of life. She needed time to heal, and was giving herself time to do it, which seemed sensible of her. But when she wasn't talking or even sometimes when she was, her eyes looked agonizingly sad to Quinn.

"You've been through a lot of trauma," Quinn said softly, and she nodded. She had no need to deny it, nor did she want to portray herself as a victim. In spite of the injuries she'd sustained, Quinn had a sense that she was both brave and strong.

"A lot of other people have been through trauma," she said sensibly, "the counseling work I do reminds me of that. Suicide is the second biggest killer of kids in this country. We have a long way to go before most people understand that. Andrew tried it twice before the last time."

"Was he on medication?" Quinn sounded sympathetic and concerned.

"Sometimes. He wasn't always willing to stay on it. He was pretty clever about pretending to take it, and then not. He didn't like the way it made him feel. It either made him feel anxious, or too lethargic. I hear a lot of that on the hotline." Quinn admired her for the volunteer work she was doing. She was a nice woman, and it was easy to see why Jack liked her. She was open and honest and not afraid to show her vulnerability. Talking to her reminded Quinn that there were others who were suffering as much as he was. He told her about Jane then. The years he had worked too hard and too much, been away most of the time, his retirement, her sudden illness, and death.

"It was all over before we knew it."

"How long has it been?" Maggie asked sympathetically.

"Nine months. She died in June. I traveled for the first five months. I've been back since November. I came back to put the house in order, and sell it this spring."

"And then what will you do?" she asked with interest. She noted that he had opted for the geographic cure, as they called it in counseling. And she didn't want to tell him that it didn't work. At some point, wherever he was, he was still going to have to face the fact that she was gone, and however he had failed her, or felt he had, whether accurate or not. Most important of all, he was going to have to forgive himself, just as she had to forgive herself, and even Charles, for Andrew's death. Unless he could, Quinn would never outrun the agony he was still feeling.

"I'm building a sailboat in Holland," Quinn explained to her, and told her about the months he had spent on the *Victory* that fall, and his decision to buy Bob Ramsay's boat and complete it. "I'm going to sail around the world for a while, maybe forever," Quinn said with a look of relief, as though he was sure that on the boat, he would no longer have to face his own demons. She could have told him different, but didn't. She knew better. But the boat he described to her sparked her imagination, and she smiled with pleasure.

"She sounds like a beauty," Maggie said with a look of admiration and nearly envy.

"Do you sail?" Quinn seemed surprised.

"I used to. I grew up in Boston, and spent my summers on the Cape. I loved to sail as a kid. I haven't in years. My husband hated boats, and Andrew never liked them much. It's been a long time."

"Jane and my daughter didn't like sailing either, especially after my son died. I had a boat years ago, when we first moved out here. But I was too busy to use it. I sold it the year after Doug died. This is going to be a rare opportunity for me to indulge my passion." He smiled at both of them. Jack was enjoying the exchange between them, glad that he had encouraged Quinn to invite Maggie to dinner. More than they knew, or even he did, they had much in common. And they were each in need of companionship and friendship. They both spent too much time alone, and had too many painful memories to dwell on. A night like this did them both good.

"A hundred and eighty feet of ketch is a lot of passion," Maggie teased him. "That must be very exciting," she said as her eyes danced.

"It is, and it will be. She'll be finished in September." He offered to show her the plans then, and they pored over them sitting at the table, as Jack cleared the dishes, and then returned to the table to join them. It was a particularly nice evening, and much to Quinn's surprise, the Friday night dinner was even more pleasant as a threesome. Maggie had definitely brought something to it, despite her heartfelt confessions. But everyone's spirits seemed to lift as Quinn described the boat in its most minute detail. Maggie asked all the right questions. She was extremely knowledgeable about sailboats, and knew of all the most important builders and naval architects and designers. Her extensive knowledge impressed Quinn considerably. And after he put the plans away, Jack suggested a game of liar's dice, which was what he and Quinn usually did at the end of their Friday evenings. Maggie laughed at the suggestion, and looked amused.

"I haven't played in years," she warned, and managed to beat them both at least once each, and then Quinn took over. He was the expert among them, and usually beat Jack as well. They had a good time nonetheless, and it was after midnight when Maggie finally left them and went home. She was scheduled to be on the teen suicide hotline at one o'clock, and she was in surprisingly good spirits.

Jack only lingered for a few minutes after she left. "She's a nice woman," he said, smiling at Quinn. "She's had a tough time. He was her only kid, and the guy who does her gardening says she found him." She hadn't told them that. "The husband doesn't sound like a great guy for leaving her after all that," Jack said, although she had described him charitably. She was a good woman, and a pretty one, and deserved to have had someone who stuck by her. It was hard for Jack to imagine the trauma they'd been through.

"People do ugly things to each other in those circumstances," Quinn said wisely. "Jane probably should have left me too. Thank God, she didn't. I wasn't very sensitive to her needs then. All I could think of was how I felt to have lost my son. I thought if I didn't talk about it, the pain would go away, instead it just went underground and ate at us both." But he had seen clearly in Jane's journals that she understood, not only her grief but his, and had allowed him to mourn in the way he needed to, on his own. She had carried the full weight of her solitary grief on her own shoulders, not unlike Maggie when she lost her son.

Jack left a few minutes later, and Quinn was in his kitchen for a long time, putting things away, and washing the dishes. And when he went upstairs finally, he saw the lights on in Maggie's kitchen, as he looked out his bedroom window. By then, he knew she was on the phone, answering the teenage hotline. Her lights were still on when he got into bed. He took out one of Jane's journals, and fell asleep holding it, but tonight for the first time, he felt more peaceful when he thought about her. However foolish and insensitive he'd been, for some reason he knew that she had truly forgiven him. Or maybe he had always known that. What he didn't know, and perhaps never would, was if he could forgive himself.

7

AT QUINN'S SUGGESTION, MAGGIE JOINED HIM AND JACK for dinner on Friday night the following week, and all three of them were in good spirits and had had a good week. They talked about the boat, and played liar's dice again. She brought a chocolate cake she had baked for them. And over the next month, their Friday night threesomes became a comfortable tradition, and an easy beginning to the weekend.

Jack's reading was going well, and he was working diligently at it. Maggie had brought Quinn some books to help him use some excellent teaching techniques that would be helpful to Jack. And Quinn showed them both the latest plans from Holland. The boat was moving ahead toward completion like lightning. It was April by then, and Jack's work was nearly finished. They had dragged it out as long as possible. Quinn had called a realtor who came to see the house. He suggested a few more things that Quinn could do to make it more appealing to a buyer, and Quinn decided to put it on the market in

May or June. He didn't want to sell it too soon, he needed somewhere to live until the boat was complete in September. The realtor felt certain the house would sell quickly, and was anxious to list it.

Quinn told Maggie and Jack about it on Friday night, and had already given Jack the list of further improvements suggested by the realtor. And this time he was able to read it. The two men had exchanged a smile about it. By then, Jack was reading with ease.

The following week, there was a heat wave, and the three of them had dinner on Friday night in Maggie's garden. She set up a picnic table, and covered it with a blue tablecloth. They ate fried chicken and hamburgers, and a potato salad Quinn had made and carried over. The evening had all the earmarks of a summer picnic. Maggie was wearing a white linen dress in the warm night air, and for once her long hair was down, cascading past her shoulders. The big announcement of the evening was that Jack said he had met a very nice young woman at his church, and the other two teased him about it. Maggie said she was happy for him, and Quinn accused her of being hopelessly romantic. Jack had just turned thirty-six, and she felt it was time for him to find someone to fall in love with. Now that he could read, he had nothing to hide, and nothing to be ashamed of. She said over dessert that she hoped he would get married and have children.

"What about you?" He turned the tables on her, as they each helped themselves to watermelon and fresh cherries for dessert.

"I've already done that," she said, giving little credence to the question. She had just turned forty-two, and was convinced her romantic life was behind her. She had been married for eighteen years before the divorce, and said she had no interest in another husband. Her son's death, and her husband's abandonment had cured her, or so she said. She claimed that she was content to live alone forever.

"You're only six years older than I am," Jack pointed out, and Quinn laughed.

"You two should get together," he suggested. Jack had already thought of it, but he hadn't wanted to spoil their friendship, and now fate had lured him in a different direction with the girl he'd met at church.

"I don't think so," Maggie said, laughing at Quinn's suggestion that she and Jack pair up. They were a loving and supportive, but definitely odd, threesome. And all three of them were sad that in a few months, their Friday night evenings would be disbanded. Quinn would be off on his boat by then, and now Jack was well on his way to having a woman in his life, if not this one, then undoubtedly another. The only plans Maggie had were to go back to teaching in September. She had spoken of it several times recently. She had nothing else to do, nowhere she wanted to go, and no one she wanted to be with. Her solitude had become a safe, comfortable cocoon to hide in, just as Quinn's was. But Maggie felt that she ought to go back to work.

The following Friday, Quinn surprised them. The weather was still warm, though not as warm as it had been the week before. But the days were long and sunny, and summer seemed to be on the way.

"What are you two doing tomorrow?" he asked innocently, but he already knew. He had planned it, although the idea had come to him on the spur of the moment, when he went to watch a sailboat race on Wednesday night, from the yacht club.

"Working for you," Jack said comfortably. He had a date planned for that night. He had already told the woman he was seeing that he was not available on Friday evenings. He called it a poker night, so he didn't have to explain Quinn or Maggie, or his reading lessons. She knew nothing about that, and he still would have been embarrassed to tell her. Maggie had told him weeks before that he didn't need to say anything. It was no one's business, although she saw his learning to read as a great accomplishment on his part, and told him he should be proud of himself.

"I thought I'd see if I can clean up my garden tomorrow," Maggie said easily. They were dining in Quinn's kitchen, as they did most of the time. He was the best cook of the group, and had the most equipment. Maggie hardly ever cooked, and lived on fruit and salads. She admitted once to both of them that she hadn't cooked since her son died, and didn't want to. The thought of cooking for anyone brought back too many memories of all she'd lost, and what her life had been. They all preferred Quinn's cooking, and he said he enjoyed it anyway.

"I have a better idea," Quinn said with a mysterious look. "I want you both here and dressed at nine o'clock tomorrow morning. Wear sneakers," he said cryptically, and Maggie laughed at him, and raised an eyebrow. She was a lovely-looking woman, although Quinn seemed not to notice. She had become like a little sister to him, and an older one to Jack.

The three of them had become family to each other. It was what they needed, more than anything else.

"If I didn't know better, Mr. Thompson, I'd think you were taking us sailing." She tried to guess what they were doing, and he laughed at her.

"My boat is in Holland. That's a long way to go for a sail. Just bring sneakers and don't ask too many questions."

"Are you sure you don't want me to do the finish work on the upstairs railings?" Jack asked, looking worried.

"It can wait," Quinn assured him. He looked immensely pleased with himself, and Maggie looked concerned.

"I hope we're not going hiking. I'm too lazy and too out of shape, and I threw my hiking boots away last winter. I swore I'd never do that again."

"Just trust me," Quinn said gently. She beat him at liar's dice that night, and went home victoriously with three dollars, to work on the hotline until three in the morning.

The next morning she rang his doorbell promptly at nine o'clock, wearing jeans, an old sweater, and a parka. The morning was cool and breezy, but brilliantly sunny. There wasn't a hint of fog on the bay, and he and Jack were already drinking coffee. She noticed when he answered the door that Quinn was wearing jeans, a heavy sweater, a thin shell, and deck shoes.

"You said sneakers," she said accusingly, as she pointed. She had worn bright red canvas sneakers, as he had said to, and a red sweater to match them, and her eyes were dancing with anticipation. "I want to know where we're going."

"All in good time, my dear. Don't be so nosy," Quinn admonished. They had come to treat each other as sister and brother.

"I feel like I'm being kidnapped," she said as she joined the two men in the kitchen and helped herself to a cup of coffee.

Their Friday nights together had made them supremely comfortable in each other's company. Maggie never bothered to dress up or wear makeup when she was with them. Her long dark hair was clean and shone in the braid she had worn. Quinn liked it when she wore it loose, but he had never said that to her. And now as he looked at her, he found himself wondering what she would look like with lipstick. She never bothered to wear that either. She wasn't trying to lure either of them. Seduction was not even remotely on her agenda.

They piled into Quinn's station wagon shortly afterward, and Maggie commented that it was the first time they had ever gone anywhere together. The physical boundaries of their relationship in the past several months had been limited to Quinn's kitchen. And she thought it was fun going out together, particularly under the mysterious circumstances Quinn had created. He was in a good mood, and seemed happy and playful, as he headed down Vallejo, and turned left on Divisadero. They were driving toward the water, and took a left along the shoreline on Marina Boulevard. Maggie wondered if they were going to cross the Golden Gate Bridge and go somewhere in Sausalito. But instead he took a right onto the grounds of the St. Francis Yacht Club. She wondered if they were going to have lunch on the deck at the club, and watch a regatta, which was the next best thing to sailing.

"This is fun," she said happily, and Jack grinned at her. She was in the front seat next to Quinn, and Jack was just behind her.

"I have a date at seven o'clock," he reminded Quinn. "I'd better be home by then, or she'll kill me."

"You'll be back before that, I promise," Quinn assured him. He parked the car and shepherded them toward the dock where the boats were, and then Maggie saw her, and instinctively she knew she'd been right. There was a splendid yacht tied up, much bigger than those that usually were tied up at the yacht club. She was smaller than the one he was building, but she was a hundred and twenty feet of sheer beauty.

Quinn walked confidently to the gangway and stepped aboard, and held out a hand to his two cohorts. "Come on, you two. She's ours for the day. Don't waste time just standing there gaping." Jack looked stunned, and Maggie looked ecstatic, as they followed him on board. A crew of four were waiting for them. She was a truly lovely sailboat. There were four cabins below, a handsome dining area on deck, and a short ladder up to an elegant little wheelhouse. And the main saloon was luxurious and comfortable, with a dining area they could use at night or in bad weather. She was named the *Molly B*, after the owner's daughter. The owner was an old friend of Quinn's, and had just brought the boat up from La Jolla for the summer. Quinn had chartered her for the day, as much to amuse Maggie as to introduce Jack to sailing.

They wandered all over the boat, as Jack looked at every tiny detail. He was impressed more than anything by the woodwork, and Maggie could hardly wait to get out on the bay and sail her. They were under way in ten minutes, and

Quinn looked every bit as happy as they did. He divided his time equally between his two friends, and was amused when Jack chatted with the stewardess, who was a pretty young girl from England. His attention to her left Quinn time to sit with the captain and Maggie and talk about sailing. The wind was perfect that day for their sail. They went out under the Golden Gate and headed toward the Farallones, and none of them minded when the water got a little choppy. Quinn was relieved to find that Jack didn't get seasick.

"You are a sneaky devil," Maggie teased Quinn as she sat on the deck next to him, enjoying the wind and sun on her face. And despite a slight chill to the wind, the weather was warm enough. "What a nice thing to do for us," she said gratefully. If she had dared, she would have thrown her arms around him and hugged him. But even after their many Friday nights together, there was always something a little daunting about him. Even at his warmest, Quinn always kept a slight distance from others. Her eyes told him how happy she was, and that was enough for him. The day had turned out precisely as he wanted.

By the time they got home that afternoon, all three of them were happy and tired. Quinn had been delighted to see that they both loved it, and couldn't stop talking about how wonderful it had been as they drove back to his house. They hated to leave each other, just as they had hated to leave the *Molly B.* Jack had thanked all of the crew members, and Quinn, profusely. Maggie didn't know how to begin to thank him. She offered to cook dinner for him, but he said he had work to do. He was still struggling through probate. It was taking forever.

Jack left them in time for his date, and Maggie thanked Quinn again before she went back to her own house, looking like a kid in her braid, white jeans, and red sweater and sneakers. Quinn smiled as he had all day, as he watched her. It was obvious to him that she loved sailing as much as she said she did. But who wouldn't, she said to him, on a boat as luxurious as the one he had chartered. She couldn't even imagine how fabulous the boat was going to be that he was building in Holland, and wished she could see it, although he had said he wouldn't be bringing it to San Francisco, except perhaps at some point, on his way to the South Pacific. But before that, he wanted to sail around Africa and Europe.

Quinn was sitting peacefully in his living room with a cup of tea, reading a sailing magazine, when Maggie rang his doorbell. She was still in her sailing clothes, her hair had come loose from its braid, and she looked slightly embarrassed.

"I don't mean to bother you," she apologized. "I just wanted to thank you." She was carrying a big covered bowl, with a loaf of French bread tucked under her arm. She had made him his favorite pasta. "I'll just leave this with you. I thought you might be hungry." He was, in fact, and had been thinking about dinner, but was too lazy and relaxed to do anything about it, so she had done it for him. "I haven't had a day like that since I was a kid," she said happily. "Thanks, Quinn. It was such a nice thing to do. You didn't have to take me, but I'm glad you did." They both smiled, remembering how much Jack had loved it. It was quite an introduction to sailing. And he had taken to it like a duck to water. He didn't even mind when it got choppy, or when they tacked or jibed, and the boat heeled as far as it could over the water. Maggie had just plain loved it, and it had reminded her of the best days of her childhood.

"You're a very efficient sailor," Quinn praised her, as he set the bowl of pasta down in his kitchen. There were tomatoes and basil and bits of sausage in it, and fresh mushrooms. She had made it for him once at her place, on a rare Friday night at her house, and he said that he loved it.

"I didn't get a chance to do much today," she said modestly, but he could tell from what she said to the crew that, given the opportunity, she knew what she was doing. And she had that look of pure glee and excitement that came over avid sailors whenever they were on a sailboat.

"We'll have to go out again sometime. My friends left the boat here, but they're in Europe." The boat belonged to yet another of his business connections. He could smell the pasta by then as he took the cover off, and as he glanced at her gratefully, he invited Maggie to join him.

"I wasn't trying to invite myself to dinner," she said, looking embarrassed. "I just wanted to thank you for a lovely day. I really enjoyed it."

"We all did. Why don't you share the pasta with me, and we can play liar's dice afterward? I need the money," he teased and she laughed. She hesitated for a minute, but he insisted, and she finally agreed to join him. He got out two plates, and they sat down easily at the kitchen table. And while he began eating, she made a salad. They talked about boats and sailing all through dinner. It was easy to see how much it meant to him. He came alive whenever he talked about boats, more than about anything else, business, or friends, or travel. He was always wistful when he spoke of Jane, and tense when he mentioned Alex. But when he talked about sailing, he seemed to relax and glow and become instantly expansive.

She was surprised by how fast the evening went with him. And by the time she finished dice with him, it was ten o'clock, and she felt guilty for keeping him from whatever he'd planned to do that night. She took her pasta bowl after she helped him clean up, and he walked her home.

"Thanks for a terrific day," she said happily, smiling up at him.

"Thanks for dinner. You owe me ten dollars," he reminded her. He had been impossible to beat that night, but she didn't mind losing to him. It had been the best day she'd had in years, surely since Andrew's death, and long before that. "Are you on the hotline tonight?" he asked, feeling comfortable with her. He always did, she was half sister and half friend. He had made a decision that night as he talked about sailing with her. He was going to wait and see how it turned out, and tell her about it the next time they met, probably the following week on Friday night. They rarely ran into each other on the street, as neither of them went out very much. Jack was the go-between, sending news and greetings back and forth during the week, since he saw both of them, and visited both houses while he worked.

"I'll be on the phone after twelve o'clock," she said easily. "I have a regular, who calls me every time I'm on. He's a sweet kid, he's fourteen. His mom died last year. He's been having a tough time. I think I'm really beginning to miss being with kids." She had already decided to go back to work in September, and had gotten her old job back, for three months at least. She was filling in for the teacher who had replaced her and was going on maternity leave. After that, the school had promised to find something for her, if they could. But it was a start, and Quinn agreed that going back to work would be healthy for her.

"Good luck on the phone tonight," he said gently. It was easy to imagine how skilled she was with kids. She had a warm, easy open way about her, and he had seen her begin to blossom slowly into the woman she had once been, ever since they'd met. Their Friday nights had benefitted all three of them, even him.

"Thanks again, Quinn," she said, and then turning to him, she threw caution to the winds, and gave him a hug. He looked surprised as she smiled at him, and a minute later, she was gone, her door was closed, and he was on his way home. Her hair had brushed his cheek, and he could smell the perfume she wore. It was a fresh airy scent that seemed so typical of her. She was like a breath of air, a summer breeze that had passed through his life, taking with it the sadness that had burdened him for so long. And he had done the same for her. He had become the anchor she had clung to when she was trying not to drown. And Jack was the glue that held them together. Quinn was grateful they had all met, and knew he would miss their company once he was gone. In five months, when his boat was finished, they would each go their separate ways, but hopefully they would be different and better than when they met. And richer for the experience. The storm that had happened on New Year's Eve, and brought them together, had proved to be a blessing for them all.

8

QUINN SHARED HIS NEWS WITH THEM THE NEXT TIME THEY dined together, as usual, on Friday night. He had chartered the *Molly B* for the entire summer, until September, when he planned to leave. And he invited them to join him on it the following weekend. This time Jack couldn't do it, he had agreed to take his new girlfriend on a picnic with some of her friends. But Maggie looked extremely enthusiastic.

"Do you mean that, Quinn? I don't want to be a nuisance or a pain in the neck. I don't want to intrude."

"I wouldn't offer it if I didn't mean it, Maggie. I'm going out on her tomorrow. Do you want to come?" Looking at him with a sheepish smile, she admitted that she did.

It was a perfect day for sailors the next day, on Saturday, when they left. She met him outside his front door, in a heavy white sweater, jeans, and her bright red sneakers, that always made her look like a kid to him. It was a cold, blustery day with a strong wind, and they took off out of the harbor at a good speed. The seas were rough that day, and he could see that Maggie loved it. The stewardess was seasick, and one of the men made lunch for them. They had sandwiches and tea, and Maggie sat smiling on the deck, next to Quinn, as they ate them. By late afternoon, the sun came out. They stayed on board for dinner, and were both happy and relaxed when they finally went home.

"You're so nice to share the boat with me. I don't know what I did to deserve all this," Maggie said gratefully as they drove home. He had changed her life with his kindness and generosity, and now with their adventures on the *Molly B*. She had no idea how to thank him, and when she said as much to him, he said he enjoyed her company. He said he was going back on the boat the next day, and invited her to come with him again. "How rude would that be?" she asked him honestly, and he laughed at her. There was something lighter and happier about his tone these days. His friendship with Jack and Maggie had lightened the load for him. He seemed happier and far less gloomy.

"Not rude at all. I can be alone on her whenever I want. I was thinking of taking her out for a couple of days this week. I don't need to be alone tomorrow. Why don't you come?" She could see in his eyes that he meant it, and she enjoyed his company too. So she went with him.

They had perfect weather and a gentle breeze. They sat in the shelter of Angel Island, and sunbathed on deck. Quinn had brought shorts with him, and she wore a bathing suit. And by the time they left the boat that night, she felt as though they had been friends forever. He started talking about Jane on the way home. He told her about the poetry Jane had written to him, most of which he hadn't seen until after her death. But when he spoke of it now, he sounded proud more than bereft. He was healthier than he had been since her death.

"It's amazing how you think you know someone, and then find out you don't," he said thoughtfully, and Maggie smiled and sighed as she looked at him as they drove home.

"I felt that way about Charles too, but not in the good way you mean. After he left, I wondered if I had ever known who he was in eighteen years of marriage. It's an odd feeling, and not a nice one, in his case. I think he hated me after Andrew died. He needed someone to blame, so he blamed me."

She had had a double trauma in losing both of them, and Quinn could only guess at what it had done to her. He had seen it in her eyes the day they met, but her divorce papers had only arrived the day before. They weren't a surprise for her, but they must have hurt anyway, and he could only guess at how much. Her husband had delivered the ultimate one-two punch, and it had decked her for a while, but she seemed to be slowly coming back to life. Quinn's friendship had been an immense source of strength and peace for her, as had Jack's. But it was Quinn who, in some ways, was the anchor of the group. Jack was the common bond they shared. And Maggie was the light and joy and fun for Quinn, far more than she guessed, or knew. He enjoyed her sunny spirit, her energy, her dry humor, and occasionally insightful wit. But more than anything, he appreciated her tenderness and compassion, which she shared with him and Jack. She was the motherly woman's touch he and Jack both needed and sometimes longed for, without even knowing it. She was Peter Pan's Wendy to the two lost boys they had both been when they all met. And now they were all getting stronger.

Maggie heard from Jack that Quinn had gone out on the boat that week, and had sailed up the coast for two days. He came home on Friday morning, and was in good spirits when they met on Friday night. He told them all about it, and reported on his own boat's progress in Holland. Everything was going according to plan, and Maggie was happy for him, although she was beginning to dread what it would be like when he was gone for good. She and Jack would still have each other, but Jack seemed to be getting serious about the woman he had met, and she knew that one day there might no longer be room, or need, in his life for her. Eventually, in their own ways, they would all have to grow up and move on. But for the moment, it was so nice the way things were.

She sailed on the *Molly B* again with Quinn that weekend, and on Sunday night when he dropped her off, he invited her to come out on the boat with him again that week. They were starting to show his house, and he didn't want to be around. It was hard to believe that it was already early May. She had nothing else to do so she agreed to go with him. She told him she was turning into a sailing bum, and loving every minute of it.

The crew left them alone most of the time, except when Quinn and Maggie wanted to chat with them. And after lunch, as they sailed peacefully down the coast, she lay on the deck near Quinn and fell asleep, and when she woke, he was sound asleep himself, lying next to her. As she looked over at him, she smiled to herself, thinking that it had been a long time since she lay next to a man, even a friend.

"What are you smiling at?" His voice was a low, gentle rumble as she lay looking at him.

"How do you know I'm smiling? Your eyes are closed," she said softly, wanting to cuddle up next to him, but she didn't want him to think she was strange. She was just hungry for human contact and affection. It had been so long since she'd had that. And the proximity to Quinn reminded her of that, and was very pleasant.

"I know everything," he said wisely, as he opened his eyes and looked at her. They were near the bow of the boat, on comfortable mattresses, lying in the sun. The crew were on the fly bridge deck, and the aft deck, and it was nice to be alone. "What were you thinking when you were smiling?" he asked, as he rolled over, and looked at her, with one arm tucked under his head. It was almost like lying in bed next to him, while wearing all their clothes.

"I was smiling because you've been so kind to me...and I love being here with you, Quinn.... I'm going to miss you next winter when you're gone."

"You'll be busy by then. You'll be teaching again." He stopped for a minute, and looked at her, and then spoke very softly in their shelter from the wind, as they lay beneath the sails. It was the perfect place to be. "I'll miss you too," he said honestly, surprised himself that he meant it.

"Will you be lonely out there all alone?" she asked, as she

moved imperceptibly closer to him. She didn't realize she'd done that, nor did he. It just seemed easier to talk.

"It's what I need," he said quietly. "I don't belong here anymore. I don't belong anywhere. My roots are gone ... like our trees that fell last winter. ... I've fallen, and I'm drifting out to sea." Just hearing that made her sad for him. She wanted to hold out a hand, but she wasn't sure it would make any difference to him. There was no holding him back, and she had no right to anyway. All she could do was watch him leave and wish him well on his travels. Their time together was limited, and destined to end soon. "I was kind of that way when I was married too. I came and went a lot, but I never really felt I belonged anywhere. I always wanted to be free. My family paid a big price for that, but I couldn't have done it otherwise. I think Jane understood it, but it must have hurt her terribly." It was what most of her poetry had been about, about letting him go, and knowing that he needed freedom more than he needed her. "I was always unhappy when I thought I was on a leash."

"And if you had no leash?" she asked quietly.

"I would sail away and probably turn up again eventually, like a bottle in the ocean, with a message in it," he said, smiling at her. He could smell her perfume again, and feel her warmth as she lay near him.

"What would the message be?" she asked gently, and without thinking, he put an arm around her and pulled her close to him, as they lay on their backs, looking up at the sky and the sails above them. There was nowhere else on earth either of them wanted to be, and no one else they would have wanted to be with. He was perfectly content lying next to her, and he hadn't felt that way in years, nor had she.

"The message would be," he said thoughtfully, pondering it, "I can't be other than I am...even if I wanted to...the message would be I love you, but I have to be free...if not, I'll die...like a fish out of the ocean, gasping for air....I need the ocean and the sky, and the fine line of the horizon with nothing on it but the sun as it goes down....That's all I want now, Maggie...wide, open, empty space. Maybe it was all I ever wanted, and I wasn't that honest with myself before. Now I have to be." And then he looked down at her with her head on his shoulder, and he smiled. "Have you ever seen the green flash when the sun goes down? It just happens for an instant, and you have to be looking at just the right time. It's the most perfect moment in any sunset, and if you blink, you miss it.... That's all I want now...that perfect instant, the green flash when the sun goes down, and night comes....I have to follow that wherever it leads me...."

"Maybe the green flash you're looking for is within you. Maybe you don't need to run as far as you think." She knew he was still running *from*, as much as he was running *to*, but only he could discover that, as she knew.

She had had her own inner battles over Andrew, and whether or not she could have changed things, or stopped him, or saved him, or was responsible for his death, as Charles had said she was. The moment had come for her finally when she knew that there was nothing she could have done. For her, the truth had come in a thousand tiny moments, like shards that formed a window she could finally look through. It came in talking to others like him, on the phone late at night, and long nights of introspection. It came in moments of prayer, and nights of bitter tears, but in the end what she had seen, as she looked into herself, had brought peace to her. She couldn't have saved him, she couldn't have changed it. All she could do was accept the fact that he was gone now, and had chosen to be. It was about acceptance and surrender, and loving someone enough to let them go forever. That had been the green flash for her, and she hoped that one day Quinn would find that too. He was still tormented about what he hadn't done, and hadn't been, and couldn't do, and until he surrendered and accepted and knew that he couldn't have changed anything, not even himself, he would have to run. It was in standing still that one found the truth, not in running, but that was impossible to explain to anyone. He had to find the answers for himself, wherever he had to go to find them, and until then he would never be free, no matter where he went to find freedom.

She looked at him then with everything she was thinking, and felt for him, and all the gratitude for all he'd done for her, and she turned her face toward him as she looked at him. And as she did, he leaned toward her and kissed her, and they hung in space for an endless instant with their eyes closed, feeling a green flash of their own. It was a moment in which two worlds gently approached each other and melted into one, and neither of them wanted the moment to end. It was a long time before he opened his eyes and looked at her. He wanted her, but knew he had to be honest with her, or whatever they shared would damage both of them.

"I have no idea what that means," he said gently, and she nodded. In the months of their friendship, she had come to understand who he was. "I'm a man with no past and no future, all I have is the present to give you. My past is worthless, my future doesn't exist yet, and probably never will, not with you. All I can give you is this moment, right now, before I leave. Is that enough for you, Maggie?" He wanted it to be, but he was afraid it wasn't. As he looked at her, he remembered all the years when Jane had looked at him with such disappointment and pain. He knew now that however much he had loved her, she had needed more of him than he had to give, and he didn't want to do that to anyone again. But this woman was different, and maybe for an hour or a moment or these few months before he left, they could share the little he had left to give. She wanted nothing more than that from him.

"It's enough, Quinn. . . . I'm in the same boat as you." The past was too painful, the future was unsure, all they had was the present moment and whatever it brought them. They had learned their lessons separately in agonizing ways, and neither of them wanted to give or get more pain than they had already endured and encountered.

"I'm leaving in September, no matter what happens between us. Do you understand that?" His voice sounded firm, and she nodded again, looking peaceful.

"I know," she whispered, and told herself that whatever did happen, no matter how much she came to love him, if she did, she would have to let him go. It was the only way to love him. Loving him meant never holding him, as well as letting him go, and she knew that to the roots of her soul.

He seemed to relax then, as he pulled her close to him. They lay side by side together, looking up at the sails, and saying nothing. There was nothing they had to say. They each had all they wanted. All they needed was to lie beside each other, looking up together, into the open sky, above the sails.

9

WHEN THE THREESOME CAME TOGETHER AGAIN ON FRI-
day night, Jack sensed something different between them, and
he couldn't figure out what it was. Quinn seemed happier and
more relaxed than he had seen him in months. And when
Maggie joined them for dinner, she was wearing her long dark
hair loose down her back. They had spent the night together
on the *Molly B* the night before. Neither of them was encum-
bered, their life and time were their own. And they were beginning to spend more and more time together on the boat.

And as usual when they played dice, most of the time
Quinn won. Jack stayed until nearly midnight, and Maggie
made a point of leaving when he did. And the following morning, she and Quinn left for the boat. They had never spent a
night in each other's house, Quinn felt very uncomfortable
about sleeping with Maggie in the bed he had shared with
Jane, so they didn't. But the *Molly B* provided neutral turf for
them, and it had begun to feel like their own. They were each

103

surprised by their shared passion. Quinn hadn't felt that way in years. And although he hadn't admitted it to her, with Maggie he felt as if he had regained his youth. With him, she had found something she had never known before. Above all, the passion and the love they shared had brought them both peace. It was a union that soothed both their souls. She wouldn't have been ready for it years before, and neither would he. But they had come together at a time that healed them both.

It was another month before Jack looked at them standing near each other one night cooking dinner, and finally figured it out. He couldn't imagine why he hadn't thought of it before. It was days later before he had the courage to mention it to Quinn.

"Did I miss something?" he asked, smiling shyly, not quite sure how to ask what he wanted to know. Quinn was still and always the elder statesman of the group. But Quinn was quick to catch his drift.

"What do you think you missed?" He smiled at the younger man. Jack was reading as though he had done so all his life, and Quinn was proud of him.

"You and Maggie? Is it what I think?"

"It could be." Quinn smiled at him and handed him a glass of wine. They had just finished their lesson, and all Quinn was doing now was polishing the gem Jack had become. They were reading Robert Frost and Shakespeare and all the poets Jane had loved, and Jack had hungered for. "I'm not sure what it is," Quinn said honestly. "Whatever it is, we're both happy with it, and that's enough for both of us." He loved the way she instinctively understood him, the way she let him be who he had to be, but at the same time respected herself. Letting him be himself was not the sacrifice for her it had been for Jane, so he had no need to feel guilty. And having lost so much in her life, Maggie expected less of him. She was tender and loving, and at the same time, independent and self-sufficient. She loved him, and was doing so with wide-open arms, which was exactly what he wanted from her. He never wanted to hurt or disappoint anyone again, as he had Jane.

"Are you in love with her?" Jack asked, looking excited, he wanted it to be that, for both of them. And he had noticed how happy Maggie looked these days. She was either singing in her garden, or happy in her house. She had blossomed like a flower in the sunshine in the past month.

"I'm not sure what that word means anymore," Quinn said, thinking about it as he looked at Jack. He had become almost like a son to him. "Love is a word that pierces men's hearts, like a poisoned dart, and then they turn and poison someone else. I don't want to do that to anyone anymore." He had understood fully in the year she'd been gone, just how badly he had hurt Jane. She had forgiven him for it, but he would never forgive himself. And he didn't want to do that to anyone again. "Heinous crimes are committed in the name of love, like holy wars. There's nothing worse."

"Don't be so hard on yourself," Jack said wisely. He knew that Quinn was.

"I have to be, Jack. If not, I'll be hard on someone else. I can't do that again, least of all to Maggie. She's had enough pain in her life." He loved her, but the last person he would admit it to was himself.

"Will you take her with you in September?" Jack asked with interest. He was pleased by the news. He thought they needed each other, and they both deserved happiness, more than most people he knew. And he loved them both.

"No, I won't," Quinn said without hesitating. He was sure of that, and had told her that from the first. She understood. "This is for now. Neither of us is asking for more than that. There's no future here." Jack was sad to hear it, but hoped they'd change their minds at some point. And he mentioned to Maggie discreetly the next day that he was pleased about what was happening with Quinn. She smiled, kissed Jack's cheek, and said nothing more. But she was glad that he knew. She had wanted to share it with him, but wasn't quite sure how. She didn't want to be indiscreet about her involvement with Quinn.

The following week was the anniversary date of Jane's death, which was hard for him. Maggie had already been through one with Andrew and knew how hard that day was. And Mother's Day, now that she'd lost her only son, was even worse. Maggie left Quinn alone in the morning of the anniversary, and went for a walk with him in the afternoon. And that night, he spent the night on the boat alone. He seemed better when he came back the next day.

The day after the anniversary, like the hand of destiny meddling in their life again, his house sold. He got the price he wanted for it, the new buyers were moving out from the East

Miracle

in the fall, and they agreed to wait for it until October 1, which worked perfectly for him. It made it more real for Maggie that he was going to leave. But she knew that anyway, and had made her peace with it, or so she said.

And in late June, he invited her to go to Holland with him, to see the boat. He had been over three or four times that spring, to check on it, but this time he wanted to show it to her. He gave her the plane ticket as a gift. She hesitated to accept it, but it was expensive for her, and Quinn knew it. He insisted that she let him invite her, and she was wildly excited when they left. They flew to London on a night flight, and from there flew to Amsterdam. He had booked a beautiful suite at the Amstel to share with her. She felt as though she had died and gone to heaven. And she could hardly wait to see the boat. After studying the plans with him for months, she wanted to see it in the flesh, and he was excited to be showing it to her. It was like taking her to his new home.

They slept for a few hours at the Amstel, and then they went to the shipyard after lunch. It was a beautiful sunny day in Amsterdam, which Quinn knew was rare. And the moment she saw the boat, Maggie caught her breath. She was speechless for a few minutes, and there were tears in her eyes. She had never seen anything as beautiful in her entire life, and it meant the world to her that he had shared it with her.

"Oh my God, Quinn, she's incredible." Seen from where she sat in dry dock, as Maggie looked up at her, she looked more like an ocean liner than a sailboat. The boat Quinn was building was huge. They rode hydraulic lifts to get on board, and Maggie was amazed at how far the interior work had gone, and it reminded her once again of how soon Quinn would leave. But she wasn't thinking of that now, she was sharing in the joy of the boat with him. He looked proud to see her so impressed. He hadn't dared to hope for a reaction as positive as this. Maggie exhibited pure, unadulterated pleasure on his behalf, and enormous admiration for him. It was a huge undertaking, and she delighted in it for him.

They spent the afternoon at the boatyard with Tem Hakker and his sons, and Quinn went over some more drawings with them. They looked forward to his visits to walk around the boat with him, and suggest improvements in the most recent plans.

Quinn and Maggie had dinner in the hotel that night, and went back to the yard at the crack of dawn the next morning. She got up early with him, and enjoyed the sights she saw on the way back to the boatyard. She was immensely grateful that Quinn had invited her to come with him. She knew that his sharing that with her was his way of demonstrating to her how much she meant to him. His excitement was tangible as he walked the boat with the Hakkers again. Maggie followed them quietly, listening to their suggestions and Quinn's. And she was amazed once again at the caliber of the work they had done.

The main saloon was wood paneled, as were all the cabins, Quinn's stateroom looked palatial to her, and all of the bathrooms were done in the finest Italian marble. And of course, the decks were teak. They were still working on the superstructure. She was going to be painted dark blue, and the superstructure was silver. He had thought of a hundred names for her, and had just settled on *Vol de Nuit,* after a book by Antoine de Saint-Exupéry, which Quinn had loved since his youth. It meant night flight, which suited the sleek look of the boat, and the purposes he intended her for. Maggie could easily imagine him sailing through the night from one exotic place to another, on his solitary adventures, much like a pilot in a night sky, beneath the stars, feeling at one with his maker. Even the color of the boat reminded her of a night sky, and the silver of the stars within it. Her name had been a long time coming. And when they left that afternoon, all of the Hakkers' most pressing questions had been answered.

They picked up their things at the hotel in the late afternoon, and got to the airport just in time to catch a plane to Paris. They had talked about spending a day in Paris but decided against it. Maggie was content with having seen the boat, which was what they had come for. They spent an hour at Charles De Gaulle, and then boarded a night flight to San Francisco. And because of the time difference, they were due to arrive in San Francisco at midnight. It had been a short trip, but a meaningful one for both of them. As they settled back in their seats, she looked at him with a long, slow smile of gratitude and kissed him.

"What was that for?" he asked, looking pleased. She had been a wonderful companion on the trip.

"For taking me to see your baby," she said, looking happy. "She's even more beautiful than I thought she'd be." She had even seen samples of his bed and table linens, flatware, crystal, and china. Everything he had chosen for the boat was exquisite. She was far more spectacular than she would have been if she'd been completed by Bob Ramsay. Quinn's taste and eye were absolutely flawless.

"Thank you for coming with me," Quinn said graciously, as he settled down in his seat, content next to Maggie. He had enjoyed sharing the boat with her. He had never known another woman with an equal passion for sailboats. And even he had to admit, this one was special. There wasn't another boat like her. It meant a lot to him that Maggie understood that. *Vol de Nuit* was going to be a yacht that no one forgot once they'd seen her. He would have loved to share her with Jane, but in his heart of hearts, he knew that she would not have appreciated or enjoyed her as much as Maggie. Sailboats had never been Jane's passion. In fact, if she'd been alive, he knew he would never have bought her. Particularly after they lost Doug, Jane had wanted nothing to do with sailboats. But she hadn't liked them even before that. It was something one was either born with or wasn't. It was rarely an acquired passion. And as it was in Quinn's, Maggie's love for boats was in her bloodstream.

They each selected movies to watch on their individual screens, and ordered dinner. They chatted quietly while they ate, about the details of the boat, and afterward, Maggie put her seat back and watched the movie till she fell asleep. Quinn looked over and saw her dozing next to him, and with a smile, he gently covered her with a blanket. It had been a whirlwind trip, and he'd accomplished a great deal, but more than that, he had come to know Maggie even better. Not just her love for boats, or understanding of the fine details of the project, what he had discovered was something far more important, and deeper. He had found the true generosity of her spirit, in being able to rejoice for him, and celebrate his accomplishment, knowing full well that the boat she'd seen was what would ultimately take him from her. She had faced her rival squarely, saluted and admired her, and was prepared to move away gracefully when he left her. It was the one thing Quinn had never found in any woman, not even Jane, and it was what made him realize now that he loved Maggie.

10

THE PLANE FROM PARIS ARRIVED IN SAN FRANCISCO slightly delayed, at one o'clock in the morning. Maggie had been asleep for most of the night, and was rested when Quinn woke her just before they landed. He had filled her customs card out for her, and handed it to her, as she smiled sleepily at him. She was sorry to be home again, and wished they had decided to spend a night in Paris. The trip seemed like a dream now. But she also knew that Quinn was busy. He had much to do before his move, and he wanted to close Jane's estate by September, which was no small project, and Maggie knew that. She followed Quinn's timetable, and was just glad he had taken her to see his sailboat.

They went through customs rapidly at that hour, and took a cab to the city. They were halfway there when he looked at her. They had no reason to go home that night, and suddenly he didn't want to. He liked sleeping next to her, and he was still reluctant to spend a night with her in either of their houses. His own still felt like Jane's house, and he realized it would until he left it.

"Would you like to sleep on the *Molly B* tonight?" he asked with a smile as he put an arm around her, and she nodded. She hadn't wanted to sleep alone that night either. She was growing accustomed to him, and missed him on the nights they didn't spend together. But she also knew that she would have to get used to it eventually. No matter how much she loved sleeping with him, and being with him, and making love with him, he would be gone soon.

"I'd love it," she said happily. She knew she would forever remember the months they were spending on the *Molly B* together.

"We can take a sail in the morning. I don't have to meet my attorney till four-thirty."

The boat was locked up tight when they arrived, but Quinn had the key for the doors and the alarm. The crew were on board, but they were undoubtedly sleeping. The first mate was on watch as they came in, and he carried their bags to Quinn's cabin, and offered them something to eat, but neither of them was hungry.

They both took showers and went to bed, and as soon as they did, Maggie nestled close to him, and he put an arm around her.

"Thank you for a wonderful trip," she whispered to him. "I think you and *Vol de Nuit* are going to be very happy with each other."

Miracle

He wanted to tell her then how much her generosity of
spirit meant to him, but for some reason, he didn't. He didn't
know what to say to her. He knew now that he was in love
with her, but it didn't change anything for him, and he didn't
want to foster false hopes or illusions. He was afraid if he told
her how he felt, she would think that he might stay, or return
for her, and he knew he couldn't. He felt he owed it to Jane
somehow to be alone, to venture on with his solitary travels.
After all he had done, and failed to do in his life, he knew he
did not deserve to spend the rest of his life with Maggie. She
was young enough to find someone else, have a wholesome
life, and forget him.

And he had never said it to her, but it concerned him that he
was twenty years older than she was. She was young enough
to be his daughter, which seemed ridiculous to him. He never
felt their age difference, but he had had his life, his children,
his career, his marriage, and now he felt he had to atone for his
sins. Indulging himself with a woman two-thirds his age, and
dragging her around the world with him seemed as selfish as
what he had done to Jane, and the egocentric life he had led,
for which Alex could not forgive him. He knew he was doing
the right thing in setting Maggie free when he left, and promis-
ing her nothing. If anything, he was going to urge her to forget
him. His mind was full of thoughts of her, his heart eased with
the warmth of her next to him, but he said nothing to her.

He was already up and dressed when she awoke the next
morning. They had left the dock at eight o'clock, and the *Molly
B* was already sailing. It was a bright June day, and as Maggie

got up, it was odd to realize that she had woken up in Amsterdam the previous morning. She smiled to herself, thinking of it, like a delicious dream, and went to join Quinn on deck in her robe and nightgown.

"Good lord, what time is it? Where am I?" she asked as she squinted at him in the sunshine. Her tousled hair cascaded down her back, just the way he liked it. She looked scarcely older than his daughter, and wasn't. There were only eight years between Maggie and Alex, but Maggie seemed an entire generation older. She had suffered a great deal in her lifetime, particularly in recent years, which made her seem far more mature, and a great deal wiser, and more compassionate certainly, than his daughter.

"It's ten o'clock. This is San Francisco Bay, you'll notice the Golden Gate straight ahead, and I'm Quinn Thompson," he teased her.

"Hello. I'm Maggie Dartman." She played the game with him. "Didn't I meet you in Amsterdam? You're the owner of that fabulous yacht, *Vol de Nuit* . . . or was I dreaming?" It all seemed like a dream now, but it wasn't.

"You must have been dreaming," he assured her. The stewardess asked Maggie what she'd like for breakfast, and Maggie smiled at how spoiled she was getting. She turned to Quinn with a grin. "To think, I used to eat Hostess Twinkies and leftover hot dogs for breakfast."

"Don't ever invite me over for breakfast. I'll stick to dinner." He grinned at her.

"Good decision," she said, as the stewardess handed her a cappuccino just the way she liked it. The crew of the *Molly B* were terrific. It was going to be tough getting used to real life again, when Quinn was gone. Because of the man, not the breakfast.

Quinn had already begun hiring his crew for *Vol de Nuit*. One was Italian, two were French, and the other seven crew members were British. He had hired John Barclay's captain from the *Victory*, after a letter he had received from him in April, asking if there might be a position for him. He had been following *Vol de Nuit's* progress with interest. Quinn had offered him the job as captain by return fax, and followed it up with a phone call. The man's name was Sean Mackenzie, and he was arriving in Amsterdam with the rest of the crew just before the sea trials in September. They were on schedule so far.

Maggie sat next to Quinn at the helm of the *Molly B* for the rest of the afternoon, and they got back to the dock at three o'clock, in time for Quinn to meet with his attorney. And before they left the boat, they agreed to spend the night on her again that evening. Both the boat and the man were becoming a dangerous habit for Maggie. The more time she spent with him, the harder it would be to see him leave in the beginning of October. He was coming back to San Francisco one last time after the sea trials, and then, she knew, it would be over. But she wouldn't allow herself to think of it, she had promised him that when he left, she would let him go without a murmur, and she had every intention of keeping her promise, no matter how hard for her, or how painful his absence. He was a gift that had come into her life unexpectedly, and when the gift was taken from her, as she knew it would be, she was going to be both gracious and graceful about it. It was all Quinn had ever asked of her, and she owed him that, or felt she did. It seemed to be her destiny to lose those she loved, to let them leave her life, no matter how costly to her.

"Are you all right?" Quinn asked her quietly, as one of the crew members drove them home, and she nodded. "You're very quiet." He had sensed something in her silence, and he wasn't wrong, but she had no intention of sharing her thoughts with him about his departure.

"Just jet-lagged," she said, smiling. "How about you?"

"I'm fine." He was still ecstatic over his visit to *Vol de Nuit*, and invigorated by it. "I wish I didn't have to meet with the attorney. I should be home by seven." They had left their bags on the boat, so she had nothing to unpack, and little to do until he came back to get her. Her life was very simple now, although she knew it would be busier once she went back to teaching in September. She was going back to work around the same time he left for the sea trials.

Jack was at the house when Quinn walked in, just finishing some work in the kitchen, and when he saw Quinn, he looked mournful.

"Something wrong?" Quinn asked with a worried frown, and Jack shook his head. He looked awful.

"I just finished."

"Finished what?" Quinn asked, looking for his briefcase with the legal folders in it.

"Everything," Jack said, and Quinn stopped and looked at him.

"Everything?" They had dragged it out as long as they could. He had been there for six months, and not only was the house impeccable in every detail, but he had become a proficient reader.

"It's all done," Jack confirmed. "We did it."

"No," Quinn said with a slow smile, as he looked at the man who had become his friend, and to whom he had become not only teacher, but mentor. "*You* did it. And don't you forget that." He walked across the room toward him and shook his hand. "We're going to have to celebrate." And Quinn meant it.

"Can I still come to dinner on Friday evenings?" He couldn't even imagine not seeing Quinn daily.

"I have a better idea. Let's talk about it in the morning. Why don't you come by for breakfast?" And then he remembered that he was going to be on the boat with Maggie. And he wanted to spend the day sailing. "I just realized I won't be here. Why don't you come for dinner on the boat on Friday night?" Jack knew where the boat was docked at the yacht club.

"Could I bring Michelle with me?" The girl he had been dating for a while had become a serious romance for him, and they were inseparable, but Quinn was hoping she was only a passing fancy. He had an important proposition to make him.

"Of course." And then Quinn thought of something. "Does she know about our special project?" Quinn didn't want to embarrass him in case she didn't.

"You mean my reading?" Quinn nodded. "I just told her. I was afraid she'd think less of me, but she thought it was terrific."

"I like her already." Quinn had not yet met her, but knew now that he would on Friday.

"How was Amsterdam?"

"Impeccable. Everything is going along at full speed. The boat looks splendid." And then as an afterthought, between the two men, "I took Maggie with me."

"I thought that might be where she was. She's been gone all week. I wasn't sure though." The two men exchanged a long look, and Jack's eyes held a single silent question, and Quinn understood him.

He shook his head. "No. Nothing's changed. She understands. She knows I'm leaving."

Jack sighed as he looked at him. He had learned a lot from Quinn in the past six months, but now he thought it was Quinn who needed to learn the lesson. "Someone like that doesn't come into your life every day, Quinn.... Whatever you do, don't lose her."

"I never had her," Quinn said quietly. "Just as she doesn't have me. People never 'have' each other." Jane had never had him, never, or at least not until after she died. And he had only found her after he lost her. He was fully prepared to give up what he had found with Maggie, and take the best of her with him, in the memories he would have of her. He didn't need more than that. He was convinced of it. "I'm too old to be romantic," Quinn said as though trying to convince himself, "or to be tied to the skirts of a woman. She understands that."

"I think you're throwing away something precious," Jack said doggedly, and Maggie would have been profoundly touched if she'd heard him.

"I'm going to give it back, Jack. That's different." Jack shook his head as Quinn picked up his briefcase and smiled at him. "See you on Friday." It was in two days, and Quinn was looking forward to it. He had no intention of giving up their Fridays, and wondered if Jack would want to bring Michelle with him every week, or keep it a threesome. Although Quinn was willing to welcome her into the group, he also loved the intimacy of the three friends, and was leaving it up to Jack.

"Think about what I said," Jack called after him, as Quinn ignored him and closed the door firmly behind him.

11

MICHELLE AND JACK APPEARED ON THE DOCK PROMPTLY at seven o'clock on Friday, and Maggie and Quinn were ready for them. The crew offered them champagne, and there were balloons and lanterns hanging on the afterdeck. It looked like a party. Quinn and Maggie had put the decorations up themselves. They had said nothing to Jack, but it was his graduation. Quinn had gotten a diploma for him and filled it out carefully with his name and the date, and had referred to him as a successful scholar. It took Jack only a moment to realize what was happening, and he was moved to tears when, at the end of dinner, Quinn handed him his diploma. Maggie had had a chance to chat with Michelle by then and was pleased to find that she liked her.

And as Quinn handed Jack the diploma he'd written out for him, the two men's eyes misted over. Quinn shook his hand, and put the other on his shoulder, and his eyes filled as he hugged him.

"Well done, my friend . . . well done. . . ." Jack was so touched he couldn't even bring himself to answer. He just nodded. No one had ever been as kind to him in his life, except Maggie. The two of them had become precious friends to him, and he knew he would never forget Quinn for the horizons he had opened. His life had been changed forever. Michelle sat watching them silently, and kissed Jack when he sat down next to her again. She was in awe of both Quinn and Maggie. She seemed very young to them. She was only twenty-four, but it was obvious that she was deeply in love with Jack, and admired him greatly.

After another round of champagne, Quinn invited Jack to walk around the deck with him, while the two women chatted. Maggie felt as though she was talking to a daughter. Michelle had just finished nursing school, and she thought Jack was her dream come true.

Jack followed Quinn up to the upper deck, and they sat looking at the stars quietly for a long moment. Quinn had been wanting to talk to Jack for some time now.

"I have an idea I wanted to share with you," Quinn began as he lit a cigar, and sat looking at the brightly lit ash for a moment. "Maybe more of a proposition, and I hope you'll accept it." It sounded important to Jack, and was, or would be, to both of them, if he agreed to do it. Quinn was counting on him, it was the greatest gift he could give him. "I've just hired the crew and the captain for the new boat. They're all coming on board in September for the sea trials, and what I was going to ask you . . . or offer you . . . was that I was hoping you would join us."

Miracle

"For the sea trials?" In spite of himself, Jack looked startled, and Quinn laughed, it was a long, low, contented rumble.

"No, my friend. As a member of *Vol de Nuit*'s crew. You could come on board as an apprentice. And if you learn to sail as fast as you've learned everything else, you'll be the captain before it's all over."

"Are you serious? About joining the crew, I mean?" For an instant, he wanted to pack his bags and run away with his beloved mentor, and then reality hit him, and he looked disappointed.

"You can do it. I know you can." Quinn had misread what he'd seen and thought he was frightened. "It will be the experience of a lifetime."

"I know it will," Jack said quietly, "or would. But I can't, Quinn."

"Why not?" Quinn looked shocked, and more than a little disappointed. He had expected Jack to think about it, and at least be tempted to do it. He was, but Quinn had changed Jack's life in more ways than he realized. Perhaps even more than he had intended.

"I'm going to college. I just got into State. I'm in a prearchitectural program. I was going to tell you tonight. And I forgot, I got so excited by my diploma. I've got a long road ahead of me. I want to be an architect one day. I could never even have thought about it without you. And I'm starting pretty late in the day. I can't take a year off to sail around the world with you, but damn, I'd have loved it." He said it with genuine emotion.

125

"I knew I shouldn't have taught you to read," Quinn said vehemently with a rueful grin, torn between pride and disappointment. He had really wanted Jack to come with him. As much as he knew it wasn't right to take Maggie with him, he would have loved to take Jack under his wing and turn him into a sailor. But he was nonetheless impressed by what he was doing. Jack had never even told him he'd applied to college.

"It'll be a long time till I graduate. I may be a hundred years old by then, but I'm going to do it. I'm going to do it at night and take as many units as I can. I'll have to keep working. And"—he hesitated for a beat—"Michelle and I just got engaged. We're going to get married at Christmas."

"Good lord, you have been busy. When did that happen?" Quinn looked genuinely amazed, and was sorry to give up the dream of Jack running away with him. It would have been like having a son on board. But he respected Jack's right to pursue his own dreams.

"It happened this week, while you were in Holland."

"Well, in that case, congratulations." He stuck out a hand and shook Jack's, but he felt a loss suddenly, as though his son were leaving home and not only going off to college, but getting married. It was a double header, and he could see now that there was no hope that Jack would join him. But Quinn was gracious about it, and as the two men walked back to join the women, Quinn looked sadly at Maggie. She hadn't known what Quinn was going to ask him, but she suspected, and she could see in his eyes that it hadn't gone the way Quinn wanted.

Miracle

"The third musketeer in our Friday night dinner club has some important announcements to share with us," he said grandly, covering the dismay he felt with a jovial demeanor, as he poured champagne for the four of them. "Jack is not only going to college," he told Maggie as she listened with affectionate interest, "he's going to State in the fall. But he and Michelle are getting married at Christmas." Jack's young fiancée blushed the moment Quinn said it, and Maggie gave an exclamation of pleasure. She kissed Jack first for his accomplishments, and then both of them for their engagement. And Quinn cheered up after another glass of champagne and a brandy. The young couple stayed until one o'clock and then left. Quinn looked sad when they went to bed that night. Maggie had already understood what was behind it.

"You wanted to take him on as crew, didn't you?" she asked gently, as Quinn came to bed in his pajamas.

"How did you know?" He looked at her in surprise, and then lay back against his pillow.

"I know you. I wondered if you might. He would have been good at it, but you've given him a life, you know. What he's doing will be wonderful for him when he's finished. You've given him what he needed to have a better life than he ever would have had before you met him. Better even than sailing." She smiled at Quinn, and had never loved him more than at that moment. She loved his vulnerability and his generosity, and his relentlessly kind spirit. In another life, it was not the way people would have described him. But this was the man she knew and had come to love, the same one who had been Jack's mentor. Not the one his former business partners had known, or even the man Jane had known, or whom his daughter hated. Quinn, as he was now, was governed by his heart, and in spite of his immense power and strength, he had been humbled, and as a result, he was even bigger than he had been. "Are you very disappointed?" she asked him.

"Selfishly, I suppose I am, but I'm glad too. I think college will be good for him. What about Michelle? Do you like her?"

"She's very sweet, and she adores him." She had seemed very young to Maggie, but so was Jack in his own way. They shared a certain innocence and naïveté, and she suspected, or at least hoped, that they'd be happy.

"It takes more than that," Quinn said wisely. "It takes so much more than that to be married." He had a profound respect now for the job he felt he had done so badly as a husband. He was his own worst critic.

"Maybe it doesn't," Maggie said kindly. "Maybe in the beginning all you have to do is trust yourself, and each other."

"I know myself far too well to ever trust myself again," he said, as he rolled over on his side and looked at her. "I trust you, though, Maggie." The way he looked at her, she was deeply touched when he said it.

"You're right to trust me. And I trust you, Quinn. Completely." All he could think of as she said it was that he wanted to tell her not to.

"I'm not sure that's wise of you. What if I hurt you?" He already knew he would, when he left her. But she had entered into the relationship willingly, knowing what the ground rules were, and what the final outcome would be.

"I don't think you will hurt me," she said honestly, "not intentionally. I'll be sad when you go, very sad. I know that. But that's different than your hurting me. You haven't lied to me, you haven't misrepresented who you are, or anything else that I know of. Those are the things that hurt people. The rest are accidents of life that no one can foresee or prevent. What you do about them is what matters. There are no guarantees between two people, Quinn. You can only do the best you can." What was killing him, and eating him up inside, was that he didn't think he had. There was no changing that now, no turning back the clock. Jane had done her best. And Maggie had, he knew from all he knew of her. But he hadn't. And Maggie's husband hadn't. And all Quinn could do was live with it now. He could never erase the pain he'd caused those who loved him. And he didn't want Maggie to be another casualty to him, even if she was willing. He wanted more than that for her, even if it meant protecting her from himself. He didn't think that he deserved her love. Nor did he feel he had deserved Jane's. Her journals, and the pain he'd read in them, were ample proof of that. "Don't be so hard on yourself," Maggie said, as she cuddled up to him in the dark.

"Why not? Don't be so generous with me," he said sadly. He was sad that Jack wasn't coming with him. Sad that he was leaving her. For all the joy he knew his boat would give him, he knew that it was not a sign of victory, but of defeat, when he finally sailed off. He knew he had failed to give Jane the best he could, and in a way, he was doing it again with Maggie. She was willing to settle for the brief time they had to share. And she was doing what he had asked her to do, to love him for a time, and then out of still more love for him, to let him go. It was the ultimate act of love, and she was willing to give him that too. He knew it was a lot to ask. In all fairness, probably too much.

"I love you, Quinn," she whispered, as she looked up at him. There was a thin sliver of moonlight that had stolen into the room, and she could see his face clearly, etched against the darkness around them. He lay silently next to her for a long time, and held her close to him. He wanted to say the same words to her, because he felt them in his heart, and he wanted to give them back to her. But the words he wanted to say to her were lodged tightly in his throat, and were unable to reach his mouth. And as he held her, and felt her hair on his cheek, there was a tear in the corner of his eye that slid slowly down his cheek.

12

JULY AND AUGUST WERE IDYLLIC FOR THEM. QUINN HAD finished most of his work on Jane's estate. He had gone through almost everything in the house, sorted it, packed it, and sent several things to Sotheby's in New York for auction. He had called Alex in Geneva several times, and asked her which pieces of furniture she wanted. She asked for only a few favorites, and a portrait of her mother, and asked him to store the rest. She said they didn't have enough room in their house for more at the moment. Each time he called, she hung up as quickly as she could. Once their business transactions were complete, she was always in a hurry to get off the phone. Quinn hadn't seen her in more than a year, since her mother's funeral, and he talked to Maggie about it one day, when they were lying on the boat, enjoying the summer sun and a late afternoon sail. They were spending most of their time on the boat these days. And Jack still came to have dinner with them every Friday night. He didn't bring Michelle with him when he came, he liked being with Quinn and Maggie on his own. But he said he was happy with her, and she was a good sport about his weekly night out with his buddies.

"What am I going to do about her?" Quinn asked Maggie about Alex. "I can't get through to her at all. She completely shut me out." He told her about the calls regarding the furniture. Once she had answered his questions, Alex thanked him for the call, and hung up as quickly as she could get off the phone.

"She'll think about it one day. Maybe when something happens to her, or something frightens her. She can't shut you out forever, Quinn, she's your daughter. She needs you, as much as you need her."

"No, she doesn't," he said, looking worried. It was yet another failure on his part, to Jane. He knew she would have been devastated to know how estranged they were especially after her death. "She has her husband and her sons. She doesn't need me."

"She's punishing you. She can't do that forever. One of these days she'll see who you really were, and even if you weren't there for her all the time, she may finally understand why you weren't."

"I'm not even sure I understand why myself. I was running all the time in those days. I thought I was building something, and I was. It was more important to me than my kids, or Jane. My priorities were all screwed up. The only thing I cared about was the empire I was building, the money I'd made, and the next deal on the table. I didn't know it then, but I entirely missed the point." As he said it, he thought of Doug and Jane,

and how swiftly life changes, and opportunities are lost forever. He finally understood that, too late.

"A lot of men do that, Quinn," Maggie said compassionately,
and for an odd moment, he wished he had been married to her
then, and not Jane. He felt instantly guilty for the thought, but
Jane had become a victim to him. After all she had suffered,
Maggie had greater insight into him, and understood far more
even than he did. She was a very different woman from the one
he'd had. "You're not the only one who's done what you did.
Wives leave men because of it sometimes, children get angry.
People feel cheated by what they didn't get. What they don't see
is what they did have, and that it was the best the man could do
at the time. You can't do it all, or be perfect for all those you love.
There are women who do the same thing these days, focus
on their careers and shortchange their families. It's hard to
keep that many balls in the air." But the ones he had dropped
were the people he had loved. He knew that now. But he also
knew that he had understood it far too late. "Why don't you invite Alex to come to the boat in Holland?"

"She hates boats," he said glumly, as he lay with his eyes
closed, stroking Maggie's hair, as she lay with her head on his
chest.

"What about her boys?"

"They're too young. They're seven and ten, and she'd never
trust me with them. Besides, I was never around for my kids at
that age. How would I know what to do with a couple of kids
that age on the boat?" The idea sounded crazy to him.

"I'll bet you'd have a lot of fun with them. They're just the
right age to teach them about sailing. And on a boat the size of

Vol de Nuit, they'd be perfectly safe. Even Alex couldn't object. The crew could help you take care of them, if you asked them to. They'd have a ball. Why don't you offer to take them on the sea trials?" He thought about it, but couldn't imagine his daughter agreeing to it, particularly after their history with Doug. Sailboats were anathema to her, but Maggie was right, of course. On a boat the size of *Vol de Nuit,* the boys would be in no danger whatsoever, unless they jumped off while the boat was under sail, which he knew they wouldn't. They were sensible and well-behaved.

"I'll think about it," he said vaguely and then turned on his side so he could kiss Maggie. "You're awfully good to me," he whispered to her, as he thought of making love to her that morning. The relationship they were developing was as smooth and warm, and spicy at times, as Maggie herself was. She was an extraordinary combination of all the things a man could want. And in the privacy of the room they shared, she inspired a passion in him that he had never known before. He was falling more and more in love with her, and yet he could never bring himself to say the words to her.

They invited Jack and Michelle on the boat for a weekend, and they sailed down the coast toward Santa Barbara. The sea was rough, and Maggie liked it that way. It seemed more exciting to her, but Michelle got seasick on the way back, and Jack apologized to Quinn for what a poor sailor she was. She still looked embarrassed when they left.

"Poor kid," Maggie said to Quinn as they sat down to dinner that night. "She's a nice girl." But she seemed very young to both of them, and Quinn was worried that she wasn't bright enough for Jack. "She'll be good for him," Maggie kept reassuring him. She could see something in her that Quinn obviously didn't. He still wished that Jack would sail on *Vol de Nuit* with him. He thought it would be the most exciting experience of his life. But Jack didn't want excitement, he wanted roots and stability and a family, and an education, all the things he'd never had, and were within his grasp now, in great part thanks to Quinn. "You've given him something much better than a cruise around the world. You've given him a shot at his dreams. No one else could have done that for him."

"All I did was teach him to read. Anyone could have done that," Quinn said modestly, but she shook her head.

"The point is, no one did." Quinn just shook his head, but he was glad that things had turned out as well as they had. It was a bond he knew they would always share. And he never forgot that it was Jack who had brought Maggie into his life. She had looked so shy and sad and scared the first time she had walked into his kitchen. And now she was flourishing, and enjoying sailing with him. He knew she was sad about her son at times, but she no longer had that look of agony in her eyes that she had had when they first met the morning after the big storm.

"That was a lucky storm for me," he said to her, when he thought about it one day. "It blew a hole in my roof, and swept you right in."

"It was even luckier for me," she said, as she kissed him.

He had had more affection from her in the past few months than he had ever dreamed of. He had had a very different relationship with Jane. Theirs had been a bond of respect and

Danielle Steel

loyalty, quiet companionship when they were together, deep affection, and Jane's endless patience. What he shared with Maggie was younger and more joyful, and far more passionate, just as Maggie was herself.

The last days of August were better than ever for them. They sailed almost constantly. And they seemed to get closer to each other with each passing day, perhaps because they knew that their final days were coming. Rather than pulling away from each other, Maggie seemed to love him with greater abandon every day, and Quinn could feel himself drifting closer and closer to her, and he no longer felt any desire to resist it. He felt safer with her than he ever had with anyone in his life. It was as though he knew deep in his heart that he could trust her in every way. And in the past month or two, his recurring dream had finally, mercifully, gone away. He still missed Jane, but differently. He felt more at peace now.

He only left Maggie when the movers came to pack up his house. He was sending whatever was left to storage. He had already sent Alex's things to her, and he was taking several suitcases of clothes and papers with him when he went to Holland for the sea trials in September. And once the house was empty, he was planning to stay on the *Molly B* until he left. It was a strange feeling watching the movers empty the house. He felt a pang every time he saw some familiar favorite piece loaded onto the truck. It was as though they were taking away the landmarks of his life. And when the house was finally empty, he stood looking around, and felt a terrible ache in his heart.

"Good-bye, Jane," he said out loud and heard his voice echo in the empty room where she had died. It was as though he

136

were leaving her there, and for the first time in fourteen months, he felt as though he were leaving her behind. He looked somber when he met Maggie back on the boat again that night.

"Are you okay?" she asked him gently, with a look of concern. He nodded, but scarcely spoke to her until after dinner that night. He was essentially living with her on the sailboat he had chartered. He would never have been as comfortable with her in his own house. He had always felt it was Jane's. And he tried to explain to her what an odd feeling it had been to watch all their belongings being taken away, and standing alone in the empty house.

"I felt that way when I moved out of the house where Andrew died. I felt as though I was leaving him there, and I hated it. I just stood there with the movers and cried. But afterward I was glad I moved to the house on Vallejo. I would never have recovered there. Charles and I had lived there. Andrew had died there. It was just too much to survive day after day. It will do you good to be on the boat," she said generously. She had still never objected to his leaving, and Quinn was impressed. She had lived up to everything she had promised. He was only sorry that he couldn't take her with him on the sea trials. He was leaving right after Labor Day, and she was going back to work the day after he left for Holland. He was coming back to San Francisco for a brief two weeks after that. And even the day before he left, he still hadn't decided what to do about Alex. Maggie kept insisting he should call her, but he hadn't. It was as though he was afraid to. It was only that night, just before they went to bed, that he sat down at his desk and called her. It was morning in Geneva.

"I got the furniture," she said matter-of-factly as soon as she heard her father's voice. "Thank you very much. It all arrived in good order. It must have cost a fortune to ship it." He had sent it air freight.

"Your mother would have wanted you to have it," he assured her. But at the mention of Jane, he could hear Alex stiffen.

"I'm happy to have her portrait," Alex mused and then she thought of something. "Where are you living?" He had just told her that everything had gone to storage. He had wanted to do it before he left for the sea trials. He wanted to spend his last two weeks in town peacefully with Maggie, without worrying about final details. And he had agreed to turn over the house to the new owners two weeks early.

"I chartered a boat for the summer. I'll stay there when I get back, I'll only be here for two weeks, before I join the boat in Holland." He had already decided to make Africa his first stop on his adventures. "Actually," he said cautiously, "that's why I called you."

"About the boat you chartered?" She sounded puzzled, but a little less icy than in their recent conversations, which seemed hopeful.

"No. I was calling about the sea trials. I'm leaving for Amsterdam tomorrow. I was wondering if you'd mind if I stop in Geneva."

"I don't own the city," she said curtly, as his heart sank.

"I'd be coming there to see you, Alex. I haven't seen the boys since last summer. They won't even know me." She was about to say that she never had, so what difference did it make, but for once, she resisted the urge to wound him. "Actually, I had an even better idea. I was wondering if...if you would like...if you'd mind...if you'd allow me to take them with me on the sea trials. You and Horst are welcome to come too, of course, but I know you're not much of a sailor. But it might be a great experience for Christian and Robert. I'd love to have them." There was an endless pause at her end. She was so taken aback, she had no idea what to answer, so for a long moment, she didn't.

"On the sea trials?" she parroted back to him. "Don't you think they're too young? You'd have to keep an eye on them every minute. And is the boat safe?" But as she asked him, the hardness seemed to drop from her voice. In spite of herself, she was touched that he wanted to take the boys. It was something she knew he would have never done before.

"I hope the boat is safe." He laughed gently in answer. "If not, I'll be in a lot of trouble when I sail on her in October. She's quite a boat, Alex. I think the boys would love her. And of course you can come too," he repeated, wanting to be sure that she knew she was welcome. But he knew just how much she hated sailboats, and for what reason. Just as Jane did, for the same reasons. She had managed to poison Alex against them. And clearly his sailing gene had not been passed on to Alex, only to Doug.

"I'll have to discuss it with Horst," she said, sounding confused about the decision. But at least she hadn't said no yet. And miraculously, he could hear something different in her voice, as she did in his.

"Why don't I call you tomorrow before I leave. I'm flying to London. It's a quick hop to Geneva, and from there to Holland." He was momentarily hopeful, although he wondered if the consultation with her husband was just a stalling tactic. He still couldn't believe she would let him take the boys to Holland with him. But he had decided Maggie was right, and it was at least worth asking. He said nothing about Maggie to her. She didn't need to know. In five weeks he and Maggie would part company, and Alex need never be the wiser that he had spent the past several months with her. It seemed disrespectful to her mother's memory to tell her, so he didn't. And when he got off the phone, he looked hopefully at Maggie. She was smiling at him.

"What did she say?"

"She said she had to talk to her husband. But she didn't hang up on me or tell me I was out of my mind and she'd rather die than let me take her children. That's something."

"I hope she lets you do it," Maggie said sincerely. And for the rest of the night, he put Alex and his grandsons out of his head, and concentrated on the woman he loved. He hated to leave her. And he wished she could come to the sea trials. They were going to put *Vol de Nuit* through all her paces. He was going to be on board for three weeks, and then come back to San Francisco. He had told Maggie to use the *Molly B* as often as she wanted, and she thanked him, but said it would make her sad to be on board without him, which touched him.

They spent a long, loving night in each other's arms, and Maggie wouldn't allow herself to think that these were almost their final moments. They had two more weeks when he got back, and even then she knew she had to release him completely. It was going to be anything but easy, but it was what she had promised him in the beginning.

Miracle

The next morning, when he got up, Quinn called Alex in Geneva. He held his breath when she answered. It was nearly dinnertime in Switzerland, and he could hear the boys in the background.

"What did Horst say?" he asked, giving her an out if she needed one. She could blame it on her husband if she refused his invitation to his grandsons.

"I...he...I asked the boys," she told him honestly in a choked voice. "They said they want to go with you," she admitted, as tears sprang to Quinn's eyes. He hadn't realized until then how much it meant to him, and how vulnerable he was to her. Although it was what he had expected from her, he knew now that it would have hurt him if she refused him. She still hadn't said yes yet, and he was almost sure she wouldn't.

"Will you let them?" he asked cautiously, praying that she would allow it. He hardly knew Christian and Robert, and this was a golden chance to do so, in a way that they would always remember.

"Yes, I will, Dad," she said quietly. It was the first gesture of trust and respect she'd shown him in her entire lifetime. All his memories of her were of anger and resentment. This was decidedly different. "Just keep an eye on them. Chris is still a baby. But Robert is very independent. Don't let him climb the masts or do anything crazy." It was the greatest gift of love she could give him, to trust him with her sons. The war between them had ended at last, or at least the first white flag had gone up.

"Do you want to come with them?" He threw caution to the winds again, by inviting her, but she was quick to decline the invitation.

"I can't. I'm six months pregnant." He was startled to hear it, and it reminded him again of how little she shared with him, almost nothing. But they had covered a lot of ground that morning. He hoped it would be the beginning of a new era in their lives.

"I'll take good care of them, I promise." He would guard them with his life, for her sake. He never wanted her to experience the tragedy that he and Jane had. And it had been Alex's tragedy too, when she lost her brother. It had traumatized her forever, and Quinn knew from Jane that his daughter was extremely cautious with her children, which made it all the more meaningful that she was trusting him with them. Particularly after all the hostility between them. It was an enormous gesture of forgiveness and confidence in him. "Thank you, Alex. You don't know what it means to me," he said, and she sounded gruff when she answered. She had thought about it all day, trying to decide what she should do about it. "I think Mom would have wanted me to do it." He wasn't sure he agreed, given how much Jane hated boats, but he wasn't going to argue the point with her. She would surely have been pleased at the rapprochement between them.

"I'll change my tickets at the airport, and be in Geneva tomorrow. I'll call and let you know what time my flight gets in, and what time we fly to Holland. You may have to meet me at the airport. We can visit when I bring them back to Geneva, if that's all right with you." He wasn't sure if he was welcome.

"I'd like that," she said quietly. His offering to take her sons with him had been some kind of epiphany for her, maybe for both of them. Other than her children and her husband, he was all she had now. "How long will they be with you?" She had forgotten to ask him before, and was surprised when he told her.

"The sea trials last three weeks, but I can get them back to you sooner, if they have school. I'll fly them in myself, if you like, or I can send a crew member with them. But I'd like to see you."

"Keep them as long as you like, Dad." It was a rare opportunity for her children, and they weren't old enough for school to make that big a difference. And she was sure her children would be crazy about their grandfather's sailboat. It must have been in their genes, they were always talking about sailing and loved boats.

"Thanks, Alex. I'll call you later." Quinn's flight was at six o'clock that night, and he still had a number of things to do before he left for the airport. Among other things, he had to sign some papers at the attorney's. And when he hung up, Maggie was waiting to hear about Alex's decision.

"What did she say?" She was looking anxious as she asked him. She had left the room for most of the conversation.

Tears filled Quinn's eyes as he answered. "They're coming with me." She threw her arms around him then and kissed him, and after that she let out a whoop of glee, and he laughed as she danced around the cabin. She was as pleased as he was. She knew what it meant to him to have evidence of his daughter's forgiveness. It was the greatest gift she could give him.

He packed his suitcase on the boat, and half an hour later, left for the attorney's office. He was meeting Maggie at her house at three that afternoon, and she was driving him to the airport. When he met her there, he was wearing a suit and tie, and carrying his briefcase. She had brought his suitcase from the boat, and they were both ready. She was wearing a short black dress and high heels, and she looked young and pretty. He hated to leave her, and said as much in the car, on the way to the airport.

"I wish you were coming with me."

"So do I," she said softly, remembering their brief trip to Holland three months before, when she had seen *Vol de Nuit* for the first time. His yacht was her only rival for his affections, but she was nonetheless a formidable opponent, and in the end, the boat would be the victor. Or rather, his freedom. And Maggie did nothing to resist it. It was a fact of life with him, and loving him, that she accepted.

At the airport, she went in with him as far as she could, and he kissed her before he left her. He told her he'd call as soon as he got to the boat, and hoped their communications system was in full operation. "If not, I'll call you from a pay phone," he teased. Or more likely, Tem Hakker's office.

"Have a wonderful time," she said generously, as she kissed him again. "Enjoy your grandsons!" she called after him, and he turned and smiled at her, and spoke in a clear strong voice as he looked her in the eyes, and nodded.

"I love you, Maggie," he said, as she stared at him. It was the first time he had said it. But she had given him so many gifts, among them the gift of suggesting that he call Alex. He wasn't going to make the same mistakes again, of keeping what he felt a secret. And besides, she had earned it. The words, so much deserved, had been hard won.

13

QUINN CALLED ALEX FROM THE FIRST-CLASS LOUNGE, and she sounded sleepy when she answered. It was one o'clock in the morning for her, and he told her quickly what time he would arrive that day, and his flight number from London. And then he told her to go back to sleep, and he hung up. He was excited to see her, and pleased for her that she was pregnant. He knew Jane would have been happy for her too. But for once, his thoughts weren't of Jane, as he sat and waited for his flight. All he could think of now was Maggie, and he was beginning to realize how hard it would be to leave her. It wasn't going to be as easy as he had thought it would be in the beginning. He was going to have to peel her from his skin like a bandage sticking to a wound. She had protected his heart for the past many months, and leaving her would expose it again. But he knew he had no choice. If he delayed his trip, it would only be worse, and he couldn't take her with him. He knew taking her would be the wrong thing to do. He had made a vow to Jane's memory. To atone for his sins and be alone. He was convinced that that was why the recurring dreams had gone. He and his conscience had made a deal, and finally made peace to honor his promise to her, or he would be devoured by guilt forever. He needed the solitude of his life on the boat, for himself, and the freedom to leave just as he had told Maggie he would in the beginning. Above all, he needed his freedom. He felt he had no right to companionship forever. He had to leave. And Maggie needed to go back to her own life, with friends and people she knew, and her teaching. He couldn't drag her around the world with him. He had to do what he had said he would. No matter how painful for both of them, he had to leave her. But for the first time in his life, he was beginning to question just how much he wanted his freedom.

But once he got on the flight to London, he felt better, and told himself it was a sign of age that he was getting so attached to her, and it would be better for both of them to end it. In a way, he perceived his love for her as weakness. And he couldn't allow himself to indulge it.

He slept on the flight, which was rare for him. And in London, he changed planes with minutes to spare. He flew into Geneva at five in the afternoon, local time, and the minute he got off the plane, he saw Alex. She was wearing her blond hair long, as Maggie did, and he was startled to realize that Maggie looked nearly as young as she did. And he was touched when he saw her pregnant. He had never seen her that way, neither with Christian nor with Robert. She walked cautiously toward him, as the boys walked a few steps behind her, carrying their backpacks, and looking almost exactly like her. They were lively little towheads, and they were jostling each other and laughing.

Alex's eyes were serious when she saw her father. "How was your flight?" she asked, without touching him. She did not reach up to kiss or hug him. She kept her arms at her side, as they looked at each other. He hadn't seen her since she left after Jane's funeral, and when she had, she hadn't even said good-bye to him. This was their first meeting.

"You look beautiful," Quinn said, smiling at her. He could barely resist the urge to hold her, but he knew the invitation to do so had to come from her, or at least the gesture.

"Thank you, Dad," she said, as tears filled her eyes, and his misted over. And then she put her arms out to him, and he folded her into his, just as he had when she was a baby, which she no longer remembered. "I missed you," she said as she choked on a sob.

"So did I, baby...so did I..." And as they stood together, the boys were swarming around them, and tugging at their mother. The moment Quinn let go of her, he had one grandson pulling at each arm, asking him a thousand questions. It surprised him to realize that both of his grandsons had Swiss accents when they spoke English. Horst and Alex spoke French to them, but their English was fluent, despite their accents. He was still holding Alex's hand, as he answered the children's questions.

They had an hour before the flight to Holland, and he suggested they go to the restaurant nearest them for an ice cream, which the boys thought was an excellent decision. They were both talking at once a mile a minute, and Alex smiled as she walked along beside her father. She looked beautiful and young and very pregnant, and for an instant Quinn wished Maggie could have seen her. He was sure they would have liked each other.

"You look great, Dad," she complimented him as she ate an ice cream with her children. Quinn ordered a cup of coffee, he was beginning to feel the two flights he'd taken so far, and the jet lag. But as he looked at her, he felt as if all the anger she had felt toward him for so long had dissipated. He didn't know where it had gone, but he was grateful for its disappearance.

Half an hour later, he boarded the plane with the boys. They would be in Amsterdam at seven-thirty, and on the boat two hours later. He had already warned the crew they were coming, and the head stewardess was going to help him watch them. He didn't want anything to happen to them. He owed Alex that much, and reassured her again just before their flight left. He told her to relax and enjoy three weeks of peace with her husband. He promised that if the boys got homesick, he would bring them back to her sooner. She was waving and wiping tears from her eyes when he last saw her. He was busy with the boys for the entire flight, and grateful for the distraction the flight attendants provided. They had coloring books and crayons for them, and brought them each a glass of fruit juice. And the boys kept him laughing and amused. Although they hadn't seen him in more than a year, they seemed to be entirely at ease with him. They wanted to know all about his new sailboat. It kept him wide awake and well entertained answering all their questions.

When they arrived in Amsterdam, they were met by the

captain and first mate, and Tem Hakker. They had brought a station wagon, and the first mate kept the boys amused all the way to the boat. Once there, they were amazed by the size of the boat, and the stewardess whisked them off to the galley for dinner.

Quinn was extremely pleased by all he could see, and he asked about a thousand details, and he was happy with all of Tem's answers. He and both his sons were coming on the sea trials with them. They had their course mapped out, and a list of maneuvers Quinn had devised to put *Vol de Nuit* through all her paces. It was nearly midnight by the time Quinn settled into his cabin, sat down with a sigh, and dialed Maggie.

"How's it going?" It was nearly three in the afternoon for her, and she had been hoping he'd call. And when he did, she was thrilled to hear him. "How are the boys?"

"Terrific. They act like they saw me last week, and they love the boat." He had gone to check on them in their cabin, and they were sound asleep by the time he got there. It was as though someone had pulled the plug on them, and their energy had shut down as they recharged their batteries. He suspected they would be up at the crack of dawn the next morning.

"How's *Vol de Nuit*?" Maggie asked excitedly.

"More beautiful than ever." He wished Maggie could see her, but he knew that wasn't going to happen, as did she. She had seen her once, and he promised to bring home lots of photographs from the sea trials.

They chatted for half an hour and Quinn gave her all the details. The boat was even more splendid than he'd expected. She looked incredible now that she was in the water. They still had to christen her, but they were going to do that at the yard when he came back in October. Tem Hakker was going to arrange a little ceremony, his wife was going to be her god-mother. He would have asked Alex to do it, but it was too hard on her to come from Geneva.

"How was Alex?" Maggie asked, sounding concerned, and Quinn smiled as he answered.

"A different woman. Maybe the one I never knew. I think she's forgiven me. Or at least she was very loving and gra-cious. I don't deserve it, but I'm grateful for it." Maggie had urged him to bridge the gap and call her, and he was grateful for that too. Her gentle hand had touched his life in a thousand ways, and the one that had brought Alex closer to him again was the most important to him. He hadn't realized until then how much he'd missed her. Seeing her was a little bit like see-ing Jane again. Alex looked strikingly like her mother, except that she was slightly taller.

"You *do* deserve it," Maggie reminded him, and then re-membered what he had said before he left her at the airport. "Thank you for what you said to me," she said, still sounding moved by it. It had been the greatest gift he could give her, and the only one she wanted.

"What did I say?" he teased her, and lay down on his bed as he talked to her. He was looking forward to the next few weeks, and also to seeing her again afterward in San Francisco. This was the trial balloon for his freedom, and the deal he had struck with his anguished dreams. He was sacrificing the love he had found with Maggie, and himself, to pay the debt he still felt he owed Jane.

"You said you loved me," she reminded him, "and you can't take that back now."

"I wasn't intending to." It still didn't change anything. He was still going to leave her. But he knew he would love her even as he did it, and maybe it was better that she knew it. He hadn't wanted to be unkind to her and strengthen their bond before he broke it, but he knew how much it meant to her, and it was the least he could do for her, to at least say it. He did love her, and she was happy to know it.

They chatted for a few more minutes and then hung up. And he was sound asleep in his new bed ten minutes later. He was utterly exhausted, but happy in his new home on *Vol de Nuit*. This was where he belonged now.

14

THE SEA TRIALS WENT EXTREMELY WELL. ALL THE SYSTEMS performed even better than expected. His grandsons had fun. The crew were more efficient than he'd hoped. And the weeks flew by like minutes. Quinn couldn't believe how fast the time had gone, and he had spoken to Maggie several times in San Francisco. She said she was exhausted and harassed, she had forgotten what teaching was like, and how boisterous her students could be, but she sounded happy and busy, and said she could hardly wait to see him. He had made a point of calling her less often than he wanted. He knew he had to start to pull away now, or it would make the final break that much more painful. And the time for that was rapidly approaching. He knew he would see her again one day, he had no intention of abandoning her completely. He would call from time to time. But he was determined not to take her into his new life with him. That had been their agreement from the beginning, and he was going to hold them both to it. As much for his sake as for Maggie's. But he was still looking forward to his last two weeks with her in San Francisco. It would be their final gift to each other.

He hated to leave the boat when he did, and the boys cried when they left the crew, but Quinn promised them they could come back as often as their parents would let them. He had a sense of the continuity of life, as he left the boat with them, and realized how much Doug had looked like Robert. Only the color of their hair was different. Jane had always said he looked like Quinn, but seeing his grandson made him realize that his son had looked a great deal like Jane, except that his hair was the color of Quinn's. But he had the impression now that his features had been his mother's. And for the first time in twenty-four years, he realized how much he missed him. He had finally allowed himself to feel it. All his pores seemed to be open these days, and Quinn nearly cried again when he saw Alex waiting for them at the airport.

He spent a night with them, and the boys regaled their parents with the tales of all their adventures. There hadn't been a single dicey moment, and the boys would long remember the trip they had spent with their grandfather. They had been beautifully behaved with everyone, and were affectionate, bright, loving children. And the next morning, before he left, Alex thanked him again, and told him how much it had meant to her to see him. It was as though all the rage had gone out of her, like an illness that had been cured, a miraculous healing she'd experienced during the year he hadn't seen her. She told him she had prayed about it.

"Will you be all right on the boat, Dad?" It seemed a lonely life to her, but he had told them again the night before that it was the life he wanted.

"I'll be more than all right," he said confidently, "I'll be extremely happy." He was sure of that now. He had been thrilled with every moment he'd spent on the boat in the past three weeks. She had more than lived up to his expectations. And his decision to spend his life on her seemed the right one to him, in spite of Maggie. Or perhaps even because of her. He felt he had no right to a new life with a woman other than Jane. Maggie had been an adventure of the heart, a moment of sunshine amidst rain, and it was time for him to continue on his solitary path now. He was absolutely certain that it was what he wanted.

He promised Alex when he left that he would try to come and see her after she had the baby. He could fly from wherever he was. He planned to be in Africa by then, enjoying the winter, and all the places he was planning to visit. He and the captain had spent hours talking about it, and Sean Mackenzie had had some excellent suggestions. Quinn was focused on that now, and a part of him had already left the life he had led recently in San Francisco.

Maggie felt it when he got back. Outwardly, he seemed to be the same as he had been when he left three weeks before, but he was already ever so subtly different. She couldn't put her finger on it, but even on her first night with him, she sensed that part of him had already escaped her. She didn't say anything about it to him, but when he held her, his embrace no longer had the passion it had had just a few weeks before. The eagle was already reaching for the skies, and preparing to leave her.

She was frantically busy at school, and trying to make time for him. They had moved onto the boat again, and she hated to do it, but she had to spend part of every evening correcting papers. She planned to give her students as few assignments as possible during his final weeks with her, but she still had to do some work. And Quinn had a lot of loose ends to tie up too. It was only when they went to bed at night that she felt they found each other again and truly connected. It was when she lay next to him with his arm around her that she felt all she had for him, and knew that he felt the same way about her. The rest of the time, Quinn seemed to have put his guard up. It was a sensible thing to do, given the fact that he was leaving her, and he hoped that would make it less painful for her. He was no longer the man he had been years before, who thought only of himself. This time he was determined not to hurt anyone more than he had to. And the last person on earth he wanted to hurt now was Maggie.

They went on easy sails over the weekend, and the weather was spectacular. It was sunny and warm, and the breeze was exactly what they wanted it to be for sailing. Jack came to dinner with them on Friday night, and he said he was loving school, and Michelle was busy planning their wedding. Quinn offered to charter a boat for their honeymoon, and Jack declined regretfully. Michelle would have hated it, since she got seasick, unlike Maggie, who would have loved it.

Their first week together on the boat was easy and comfortable, Quinn and Maggie managed to make time for each other, and they spent a lot of time talking at night, as though storing memories to save for the many years ahead when they would no longer be together. Waiting for him to leave was like planning a death, or a funeral. They knew it was coming, and even when. She felt as though he were going to pull the plug on her respirator, and even though she had always known it would come to this, she had never expected it to hurt quite so acutely.

By the second week, the anticipated end began to cause both friction and tension between them. It was impossible for it not to. Maggie began dreaming of Andrew every night, and she had a nightmare about Charles, and woke up screaming. And there was very little Quinn could do to help her. All he could have done was change his plans, and decide not to leave, and Maggie would never have expected that of him. But nonetheless, as the days rolled by, she felt as though the life and air were being sucked out of her. She could hardly breathe on their last weekend, and Quinn was feeling the full weight of what it was doing to her, although she never said anything about it. He knew he had to leave her, even though for a crazed instant he almost asked her to come along. But he owed more than that to Jane. And Maggie needed a real life again, with people and friends and work. He couldn't just abscond with her on a boat. And if he took her with him, however tempting that was, he would have broken his vow to Jane. He said as much to Maggie again as they sat on the aft deck under the sails. She was looking miserably unhappy, and could no longer conceal it, nor tried.

"I can't believe she'd have expected that of you," Maggie said, looking out to sea, and feeling as though she were about to scatter her own ashes. "I read her poems to you. She loved you, Quinn. She wouldn't have wanted you to be unhappy."

And the odd thing was, he wasn't. He was sad to be leaving her, but there was a certain sense of peace to be going to solitude and freedom, almost like a monastic life he had chosen. He needed the respite he knew it would give his soul. He no longer had the energy to begin a life with anyone, and he hadn't earned it. He had made too big a botch of the last one, as far as he was concerned. And he didn't want to make a mess of it with Maggie, he didn't want to risk it. He loved her too much to hurt her. They had each suffered enough pain in their lives. He wanted to leave her knowing that he had made her happy. They had been good to each other, and he didn't want more than that from her, nor did he feel he could give her more than he had. They had done it, and loved well. And now it was time to end it. On Monday, he was leaving for Holland. All that remained to them now was one final weekend. Jack came to dinner on Friday night, and he and Quinn said good-bye with a warm hug and a powerful handshake.

On Sunday, Maggie was agonizingly silent. She could barely talk to him. There was nothing left to say. It had all been said a thousand times, a thousand ways. She wished that she had had Jane's gift with poems. But all she felt in her heart now was pain, the agony of loss she had already felt too often for one lifetime.

Quinn lay next to her on the deck, and held her hand. They lay there for a long, long time, and the crew left them alone, knowing what was coming. Quinn had ordered a sumptuous dinner for them, with caviar and champagne, and Maggie barely touched it. And shortly afterward, they went to their cabin. It was then that she began to cry, and looked at him with eyes that tore his heart out. It almost made him regret coming back after the sea trials. This was too hard for both of them, and he wondered if he had made a mistake coming back to San Francisco, if that had been even crueler to her. But however they had done it, or when, the end would have been excruciatingly painful.

Before they went to bed, she stood in her nightgown and said the words he had dreaded hearing. "Quinn, please take me with you."

"I can't, Maggie. You know that," he said sadly.

"No, I don't. It doesn't make sense to me. I don't understand why we have to do this." Tears were rolling down her cheeks in silent rivers.

"We agreed to this in the beginning," he reminded her. "You know that."

"That was then, and this is different. We didn't know we'd love each other then. I love you, Quinn."

"I love you too, Maggie. But sooner or later, I would hurt you." He wanted to add that he didn't deserve her, but he stopped himself. That was the flaw in all of it. He still felt he had to atone for his past sins. Alex had forgiven him. And Jane would have, Maggie was sure. But Quinn couldn't forgive himself. And as long as he didn't, he couldn't allow himself to be happy. He had to find solitude to atone for all that he could never change now, and he wanted Maggie to understand that. "I've hurt everyone I've ever cared about. My daughter, my son, Jane. . . . How can I forget all that? Can't you understand that?" In Maggie's eyes, he was like Charles, unable to forgive himself for what had happened. And he had also blamed her. Quinn blamed only himself. And whatever their reasons for leaving, whether it was Andrew, Charles, or Quinn, she was the loser.

"You can't run away forever, Quinn," she said, looking agonized.

"Yes, I can," he said sadly. "I ran away in the past, and it was the wrong thing then. But this time it's right, Maggie, I know it. You'll have a better life without me." There was no reasoning with him. He was convinced that he was doing the right thing, and it was what he wanted. Maggie couldn't sway him. He would not let her.

"I don't want a better life. I want to be with you. You don't have to marry me, or betray Jane. You can stay married to her forever. I just want to be with you. How can you throw this away, or walk away? It's totally crazy." It made no sense to her now, particularly because she knew he loved her. But to Quinn, that was all the more reason to leave her. It was what he expected of himself. He owed this final sacrifice to all the people he had hurt in the past, whether or not Maggie understood it.

In the end, she lay and sobbed in his arms for most of the night, and in the morning they both looked as though someone had died. It took every ounce of courage she had to dress and follow him upstairs to breakfast. She just sat silently with tears rolling down her cheeks, as he looked at her, as bereft as she was. She hadn't felt this awful since Andrew had died, and that had made just as little sense to her. Her beautiful child had taken his life. And now this man was leaving her because he loved her.

"This is what I believe is right," Quinn said quietly. "Please don't make it harder than it already is." And out of sheer love for him, she nodded, and at least tried to pull herself together. He had already told her that he didn't want her to take him to the airport. And she knew she couldn't. He held her for a last time, and kissed her, storing the memories for himself, and she touched his face one last time before he put her in a cab. His was coming in a few minutes.

As she pulled away, he stood on the deck watching her. Their eyes never left each other for a single moment. He raised his hand once and waved at her. She blew him a kiss as the cab pulled away, and as soon as they were out of sight of the boat, she was engulfed in sobs, and the driver watched her silently in the rearview mirror. She had him take her home, and didn't go to work that day. She couldn't. She sat in her kitchen, watching the clock. And when she knew his plane had taken off, she put her head down on the table and sobbed. She sat there for hours, crying and never moving. She had cherished the months she spent with him, and now she knew she had to do what she had promised, no matter how painful. She had to let him go, to be how and where and what he wanted, whether or not it made sense to her. If she loved him as she said she had, she had to let him have the one thing he wanted of her. His freedom.

She sat with her eyes closed for a long, long time, thinking of him, and willing him to be as free as he wanted. And as she did, his plane circled slowly over the bay, and headed north toward Europe. He was looking down at the Golden Gate Bridge as they flew over it, as tears slid silently down his cheeks.

15

FOR THE NEXT SEVERAL WEEKS, MAGGIE FELT AS SHE HAD when Andrew died. She moved through the days as though swimming underwater. She had no energy, she never smiled, she hardly slept at night, and when people spoke to her, she barely heard them. She felt disconnected from her entire world, as though she had fallen from another planet, and no longer spoke the language or understood the words people spoke to her. She lost her ability to decode the world around her. She went to work and was painfully distracted. She could barely manage to give assignments and correct papers. All she wanted to do was stay home, and think of the time they had shared. Each remembered moment now seemed even more precious.

The only useful thing she did was volunteer again for the teen suicide hotline. She had taken two months off from it over the summer. But since she couldn't sleep at night anyway, it seemed like a worthwhile use of her time. But she was just as depressed as her clients, although she made an effort to sound normal when she spoke to them. But nothing about her life seemed rational or normal to her anymore. Quinn leaving had opened up the wound of loss again, and reminded her of everyone she'd ever loved and lost. She felt as though yet one more person she loved had died. At times, she felt as though she had died herself.

She had dinner with Jack on Friday night. She hadn't wanted to, but he had called her that morning and insisted. She thought seeing him might remind her of Quinn. The bond to Jack was another valuable gift he had given her. And Jack looked almost as depressed as she did. He said he really missed him. Quinn had shared so much with them, and given of himself so freely, and yet she knew he couldn't forgive himself for past sins. She had his Satcom number on the boat, for emergencies, but she had promised herself not to call him. He had a right to the freedom he so desperately wanted. And she would give it to him now, no matter what it cost her. But the rest of her life stretched ahead of her like an empty desert. Jack said he had been so upset the night before that he and Michelle had had an argument about their wedding. And now he was sorry that he hadn't gone with him.

"At least he invited you," Maggie said ruefully. They had both cried at the beginning of dinner.

"Every time I read something, I think about him." He told Maggie then that college was hard, but he loved it, and he still wanted to go to graduate school in architecture when he finished. And he was determined enough to do it. "I'm going to be the oldest architect in San Francisco," he said, and they both smiled.

It was nearly Christmas before Maggie felt halfway human. She and Jack had continued to have their Friday night dinners, although they no longer played liar's dice. It reminded them both too much of Quinn. Instead, they sat and talked about him. It was the only time when Maggie could indulge herself and do that. No one at the school where she taught knew anything about him. Jack said Michelle was sick and tired of hearing about him. Their wedding was scheduled for the week before Christmas. Maggie had promised to attend, but she wasn't in the mood for it. She hadn't bothered to buy a dress, and pulled a short black dress out of her closet the afternoon of the wedding. Jack had told her a few days before that he'd had a postcard from Quinn. He had flown back from Cape Town, to see Alex and the boys in Geneva. Jack had brought the card with him, and asked Maggie if she wanted to see it, but she didn't. It would just make her cry again, and there was no point in that. She had cried endlessly in the past two months. Her gift to him was to free him.

She went to Jack's wedding that afternoon, cried copiously during the ceremony, and felt morbidly depressed during the reception. She didn't want to dance with anyone. She just wanted to go home, to be alone, and think about Quinn. She was trying to pull out of it, but after Andrew's death, it had become increasingly difficult to lose anyone or anything. And losing Quinn was a loss of such magnitude that it had reopened all her other wounds. But no matter how painful it was for her, she knew she had to survive it. She owed Quinn that.

And as soon as it seemed respectable to her, she slipped away from the wedding. It was a relief to go home, and escape the noise and food and revelry. It had been good to see Jack happy again, and Michelle looked beautiful and ecstatic. Maggie was sure they would be very happy.

It was only on Christmas Eve that she began to find a sense of peace about what had happened. Instead of looking at the years she wouldn't share with him, she thought of the months she had, what a blessing they had been for her, and how lucky she was to have known him. Just as she had done two and a half years before with Andrew. She concentrated on gratitude instead of loss, and she thought of calling him on Christmas morning, and after wrestling with herself for two hours, she managed not to. She knew that if he wanted to talk to her, he would have called her, and he didn't. All she could do now was wish him well, and cherish the memories. And there were many of them. It was enough for her, it had to be. She had no choice but to go forward, with or without him. And when she went to church on Christmas Eve, she lit a candle for him.

16

ON CHRISTMAS EVE, QUINN WAS IN GENEVA WITH ALEX and her family. He went to midnight Mass with them, and in the long-forgotten tradition of his youth, he lit a candle for Maggie.

Alex had had the baby two weeks before, and as he had promised her he would, he had come to see her. It was something he knew Jane would have done, and he did it for her, since she couldn't.

Alex had had a girl this time, and the boys were fascinated by her. They were constantly holding and touching and kissing her. And Alex was remarkably relaxed when they nearly dropped her. She was happy to have some time with her father. He sat with her quietly and talked, while she nursed the baby. And being there with her reminded him of the many times when he hadn't managed to come home from some far corner of the world for Christmas. He apologized to her, and she said she understood it. It meant a lot to her that he had flown in from Cape Town just to see her. He had left the boat there, and was flying back to it on Christmas morning.

Quinn had spent a week with them, and as he sat with Alex after Mass that night, he was tempted to tell her about Maggie, but decided he shouldn't. He still felt he had done the right thing, but was surprised by how much he had missed her in the two months since he left her. Their attachment had been greater than even he had understood, and he couldn't help wondering what Alex would think about it. But he didn't have the courage to tell her. He felt sure that she would view it as a betrayal of her mother.

He still loved Jane, and thought about her, but it was Maggie who came to mind constantly, as he sat on deck at night and looked at the ocean. Jane seemed more like part of the distant past, and Maggie was integrally woven into the fabric of the present. But no longer the future. Whatever future he had would be spent alone on *Vol de Nuit*, contemplating his failures and victories, and the people he had loved and who were no longer with him.

He was grateful that Alex was no longer part of his past, but had come into his present. He kissed all of them, and left presents for everyone, when he left early on Christmas morning. He had spent a week with them, and didn't want to intrude on them. He thought they should spend Christmas together, and holidays were painful for him now anyway. In truth, he had never really liked them.

He flew back to Cape Town, and it was late that night when he joined the boat again. It was a great relief to be there. *Vol de Nuit* was home now.

They sat in port for another three days provisioning, and Quinn spent hours with the captain charting their route. They were going to sail around the Cape of Good Hope, and travel up the east side of Africa. There were places where it seemed unwise to go with a yacht the size of *Vol de Nuit*. He didn't want to enter hostile areas, or expose the crew to unnecessary danger. And by the time they set sail again, Quinn was happy to be sailing and heading for new locations.

The weather began getting worse after the holidays, and in the second week of January, it began raining. They had three days of heavy rains and rough seas, and Quinn couldn't help remembering the storm of a year before in San Francisco. It was in the aftermath of it, on New Year's Day, that he had first seen Maggie, standing in the pouring rain, with everything she was wearing soaking wet. And as he thought of it, he was tempted to call her, but resisted. Hearing her now, and talking to her, would just be painful for both of them. He was determined to let her go. He wanted her to have a better life than he felt he could give her.

They changed their course after a week of rain, and by the second week, the entire crew was tired of it, and so was Quinn. They got out their charts and began mapping a new course, hoping to find better weather, but it was worse instead. *Vol de Nuit* was pitching and rolling in heavy seas. Everyone but Quinn and the captain was sick, and Quinn jokingly said they'd have to lash the crew to their beds if the weather didn't get better. He was in his bed that night when he heard a crash. The seas were so rough that a piece of furniture had broken loose and fallen over. He looked at the gauges next to his bed, and saw that the winds had reached gale force. He put on his clothes and made his way to the bridge to talk to the captain. Their new course seemed to have taken them into the worst of the storm. Quinn was startled by the size of the waves breaking over the deck when he met the first mate, the engineer, and the captain in the wheelhouse. They were looking over the weather reports and watching the radar. There was green water sweeping over the deck, and the waves were crashing over the wheelhouse. And each time the bow dove down and came up again, it felt as though the masts would break, but Quinn was sure that they wouldn't.

"Looks like we're rock and rolling," Quinn said cheerfully, but he was shocked to see that the captain looked worried. "How're we doing?" Quinn didn't expect to have any problems. *Vol de Nuit* was sound and able to withstand almost any weather, and conditions, and rough seas had never frightened him. They just had to get through it. And Quinn was never seasick.

"There are some nasty reefs out there," the captain said, after carefully examining their radar and sonar. "And there's a tanker in trouble. The navy responded to them a while ago, but it looks like things are going to get worse before they get better."

"Looks like a hurricane, doesn't it?" Quinn said, as though it wasn't happening to them. And then a moment later, he turned to the captain. "I want the men in harnesses. Have we got the safety lines up yet?"

"We put them up an hour ago," he said reassuringly. They

wore harnesses with lights on them, and clipped the safety lines to their harnesses in case they got swept overboard, but Quinn knew that if anyone went over the side in waves like this, it would be almost impossible to retrieve them.

"Tell them to be careful," Quinn said to the first mate, and started out on deck to see how the crew were doing. Everyone had yellow foul weather gear on, including Quinn, and the captain told him sternly to put a harness on before he left the wheelhouse. "Yes, sir." Quinn smiled at him, and was glad that Sean was being careful.

Quinn put the harness on and went outside to join the other men. And as he did, there were some nasty crashing sounds in the galley. The boat was shuddering by then, and the only thing Quinn was worried about was breaking a mast. There was nothing they could do at this point, but ride through it. But it was unsettling for everyone, and as Quinn watched the waves, he was genuinely concerned for the first time. They were the roughest seas he'd ever seen. The waves were as tall as skyscrapers, towering seventy or eighty feet above them. It would have been a challenge to any ship, and was to *Vol de Nuit,* and as he stood looking into the darkness, he heard a shout a few feet away from him. One of the younger crew members had nearly gone over the side, and two of the other men had grabbed him. They were clinging to the safety lines, and all three of them looked like they were going to be swept off the boat as the sailboat dropped straight down into a giant trough. It was an eternity before they rose again and the mammoth waves crashed over them.

"Get everyone inside!" Quinn shouted and gesticulated at them through the wind, and the men began slowly crawling back up the boat, the deck was at a nearly-ninety-degree angle, and it seemed a lifetime before the crew were crowded into the wheelhouse, dripping water. It was the first time in his life that Quinn had been truly worried on a boat, but he'd never seen a storm like this one, except in movies. They had tied down everything they could, but things all over the boat were crashing and breaking. He wasn't worried about the damage now, but only their survival, and most of the men looked genuinely frightened. "Well, this will be one to talk about," Quinn said to ease the tension, and the entire boat seemed to groan and shudder as they headed down into the trough of the next wave. Quinn didn't want to let on to them that even he was frightened, and he bitterly regretted the course they'd taken. It had been a calculated guess on his part, but clearly it had been the wrong one. There was nothing they could do now but ride it out, and pray they'd make it.

Morning dawned grim and gray again, and the waves only seemed to get bigger, the wind worse. The two stewardesses had joined them in the wheelhouse by then, and reluctantly the captain told everyone to put life vests on. There seemed to be a distinct possibility that they might not make it.

They radioed to the nearest ship, and were told that the tanker had gone down, and no one had made it into the lifeboats. There would have been no point anyway. No one could have survived this. Shortly after nine o'clock there was another distress call on the emergency frequency. A fleet of fish-ing boats had gone down. Quinn and the captain exchanged a long look, and somewhere in the wheelhouse, a crew member was praying out loud. Quinn suspected that silently, they all were. He would have offered them something to fortify them and keep their spirits up, as they'd been up all night, but they needed to keep their wits about them.

He stood at the windows watching the waves again, and as he stared into the driving rain, he could have sworn he saw a woman's face, and it was Maggie. And as he thought of her, and the time they had spent together, he had an overwhelming urge to call her, and promised himself he would, if they survived the storm, which was beginning to seem less and less likely. *Vol de Nuit* could only stand so much abuse, and the waves seemed to be getting bigger instead of smaller. There was a deafening silence in the wheelhouse, and the only sounds were those of furniture falling below, and another series of crashes in the galley.

"Well, guys," Quinn said quietly, "we're in it this time. But I'd like to keep the boat. I spent a hell of a lot of money on her." The engineer laughed a hollow sound, and a few minutes later, the rest of the crew started talking. They were telling war stories about storms they'd been in, and Quinn did the best he could to keep the conversation going, but you could smell terror on their skins, and the sight of all of them in life vests was anything but reassuring. Some of the men had lit cigarettes, and a few were still not talking. Quinn was sure that they were praying, and through it all, as he talked to them, he kept thinking of Maggie. This seemed a hell of a way to die, but in a way this was what he had wanted, to end his life at sea one day. It was just happening sooner than he had expected. He was glad she wasn't there, the last thing he would have wanted to do was kill her. And both of the stewardesses were crying.

This time, when the boat crashed down, two of the men started singing, and the others slowly joined them. If they were going to die, they were going to go like men, with guts and style. They were a brave band as the storm raged on. It seemed like an eternity, but by noon, they were moving ever so slowly into calmer waters. The storm continued to rage on, but the waves were not quite as ominous, and the boat wasn't shaking quite as badly. It was nightfall before the rain and wind began to slow down. The damage inside the boat was considerable, but they were in reasonably manageable circumstances again by midnight. The boat was still pitching and rolling, but Quinn and the captain agreed they were no longer in grave danger, and by morning, they were both certain they were going to make it. They motored into port in Durban early that afternoon with a cheer of victory and tears rolling down their faces.

"We'll remember that one," the captain said quietly to Quinn, and he nodded, looking grim. He had spent nearly two days thinking of what he had done with his life, as they all had. More than fifty men had died the night before, and Quinn was profoundly grateful that they hadn't been among them. It was a storm that all of them would remember for a lifetime. And as they motored slowly into port, and docked the giant sailboat, Quinn turned to the captain and thanked him. They had already agreed that they would have to get *Vol de Nuit* back to

Holland for repairs. But all that mattered was that all of the crew were alive. By sheer miracle, the boat had survived and they had lost no one. Both Quinn and the captain had been certain at one point that the boat would go down. It was a real miracle that she hadn't. And for the first time in his life, Quinn knew without a doubt that nothing but a miracle could have saved them.

17

MAGGIE WOKE UP TO THE SOUNDS OF A DRIVING RAIN ON
her windows. She had been awake most of the night, unable to
sleep, thinking of things she had to do that day, and papers she
had to grade by the following morning. She was beginning to
enjoy her work again. And she had saved a fourteen-year-old
girl two nights before on the hotline. Her life was beginning to
make sense again, although she couldn't say that she was enjoying it. But her mind was clear, and her heart was not constantly as heavy. Only when she thought about him. But she
knew that in time, she'd survive it. She had done it before and
would again. Eventually, the heart repairs. She had learned
that with Andrew. The scars and memories remained, but in
time, one learned to live with the damage, and even function
in spite of it. She couldn't let losing Quinn destroy her life. She
had no choice but to survive it. If not, everything she said to
kids on the hotline was a lie, and she couldn't allow that to
happen to her. If she could give them a reason to live, she had

to find one. She couldn't allow herself to mourn him forever. She couldn't afford it.

She got up and showered and dressed for school. She drank a cup of coffee, and ate a piece of toast, and half a grapefruit. She put her raincoat on and went out in the rain. And she was running toward her car, with her long braid flying out behind her, and the rain beating down, as she saw a man dart toward her. She couldn't imagine what he was doing, and she had her head down in the wind and rain, when he reached out for her and she jumped away. It was a crazy hour of the day for someone to attack her. But all he did was wrap his arms around her as she tried to push away, and he just stood there and held her. He had knocked the wind out of her, and she tried to catch her breath as she struggled to look up at him, and then she saw him. His hair was short, his face was lean, and he was as wet as she was. He was just standing there holding her. It was Quinn, or someone who looked just like him.

"What are you doing here?" she asked with a look of amazement. He was in Africa somewhere, or he was supposed to be, and now he was here with his arms around her.

"The boat almost went down in a storm off the coast of Africa. I just took her to Holland for repairs," he said, sounding as out of breath as she was. She pulled away from him then, and looked up at him, as the rain beat down on both of them. He looked wild-eyed and exhausted, and she guessed that he must have just gotten off a plane. He looked as though he hadn't slept in days, and he hadn't. "I saw your face in the storm when I thought we were going down. I swore that if we survived it, I'd call you." She looked suspicious of him. She had suffered the agonies of the damned since she last saw him.

"You didn't call me," she said as though that made sense. But nothing did now. She didn't know why he was here, or what he was saying. It was as though he was speaking to her in a foreign language. Her mind was racing.

"No, I didn't." There was something in his eyes she had never seen there when he was with her. Something powerful and strong and sure. It was as though he had died and been born again. He had, and was free now. "I wanted to see you. Are you all right?" She nodded, remembering how powerful his arms had just seemed around her. She had thought he was going to kill her. And losing him nearly had. But like him, she had faced the storm he'd left her in and survived it. They stood there in the rain, looking at each other, trying to see what was left, if anything. They had been washed over the side by forces stronger than they were, and had no idea if they could get back. "I had a dream about Jane, on the way back to Holland. She seemed so peaceful. She told me she was fine and that she loved me. And at the end of the dream, she just smiled and walked away." Maggie listened to him and nodded. They both knew what it meant. Forgiveness at last.

"I'm late for school," she said, for lack of something better to say, and he appeared not to hear her.

"Will you come with me?" He had come six thousand miles to ask her that question. Farther than that. He had come from the bowels of death and across his entire lifetime. But the one thing he had found in the storm was all he needed. In the jaws of death, he had found forgiveness. He knew that if he had been saved, then he deserved her. It was why he had seen her face that night, as though she had been a vision and a promise. He had found what he'd been looking for, not only forgiveness, but freedom. He had paid his dues to the utmost farthing. And the final dream of Jane had set him free at last.

"Are you serious?" She stared at him as though she didn't believe he meant it.

"I am. Are you? Do you want to come with me?" She hesitated for what seemed like an eternity to him, and then finally, she nodded.

"I do. Do you still want me?" she whispered, and he laughed this time.

"I damn near went down with the boat, and God knows why we were saved, me most of all. And I came from Africa to Holland to New York to here. Yes, Maggie, I want you. More than that, I am the biggest fool that ever lived, I used to be the biggest sonofabitch that ever breathed. And I promise you, I'll never leave you again. Oh yes, I will, but not the way I did in October. I guess I needed to damn near die to figure out what I really wanted." He got down on bended knee in the rain and she laughed at him. "Now, will you come with me?"

"Okay, okay. But I have to give them notice at school. And I have to grade papers. How soon are you leaving?"

"I'm not leaving till you come with me. The boat will be in Holland for at least two months, maybe three. Can I stay with you?" he asked, as she smiled up at him. He had never looked better to her. And she looked every bit as good to him, and just as soaking wet, as she had the day he met her. "Do you want me to drive you to school?" She smiled up at him and nodded. "How soon can you give them notice?" he asked as she handed him her car keys. This was all so wonderful and so crazy, just as he was. He had come halfway around the world to ask her to leave with him, and he had to nearly die to do it. But if that was what it took, it was worth it.

"I'll give them notice today. Will that work for you?" she asked as he started the car and backed out of the driveway. They were both wet to the bone as he stopped the car again and looked at her.

"Did I tell you I love you?"

"I can't remember. But I figured it out anyway. If you came all this way, I thought you probably did. I love you too. Now get me to school, I'm late. You scared the hell out of me. I thought you were trying to attack me."

"I was just glad to see you." He grinned at her, backed the car the rest of the way out of the driveway, and drove the car down Vallejo. She agreed with him as he told her about the storm they'd been in. It was a miracle. It had taken a miracle to bring him back to her. And she reminded him, as she leaned over and kissed him, that it had been a storm that brought them together in the first place.

He dropped her off at school, and she waved at him, as he sat and watched her run through the rain. She was the miracle that had come into his life, and brought forgiveness. And love was the miracle that had healed him.